I CORINTHIANS

CALLED INTO FELLOWSHIP

God is faithful, by whom ye have been called into the fellowship of his Son Jesus Christ our Lord.

—I Corinthians 1:9

I CORINTHIANS

CALLED INTO FELLOWSHIP

Stephen Kaung

Christian Fellowship Publishers, Inc.
New York

Paperback ISBN: 978-1-68062-127-3
eBook ISBN: 978-1-68062-128-0

Available from the Publishers at:

11515 Allecingie Parkway
Richmond, Virginia 23235
www.c-f-p.com

Printed in the United States of America

Contents

In 2007 nine messages on I Corinthians were delivered by the author before a group of Christians gathered together in Richmond, VA. The texts of these messages were recorded and later transcribed and lightly edited for publication.

Unless otherwise indicated,
Scripture quotations are from the
New Translation by J. N. Darby.

1—The Fellowship of His Son

1 Corinthians 1:9—God is faithful, by whom ye have been called into the fellowship of his Son Jesus Christ our Lord.

At the beginning of this first letter to the Corinthians, the apostle Paul gave us a tremendous statement. The more I meditate on it, the more I marvel at it. He said, "God is faithful, by whom ye have been called into the fellowship of his Son Jesus Christ our Lord." I hope we do not just let this statement pass carelessly. It is a marvelous, glorious, way-beyond-our-thoughts statement, which is eternally true.

God is faithful,

by whom ye have been called

Whether we are faithful or not does not matter. He remains faithful. And He is faithful to one thing—His calling: "by whom ye have been called." He calls us "into the fellowship of his Son Jesus Christ." Can you think of anything nobler, higher, more heavenly, more spiritual, or perfect than to be called into the fellowship of God's Son Jesus Christ?

Thank God, this statement not only applies to the Corinthian believers, but it applies even to us. Again, at the start of this letter it says:

to the assembly of God which is in Corinth, to those sanctified in Christ Jesus, called saints, with all that in every place call on the name of our Lord Jesus Christ, both theirs and ours (1:2).

Notice how this letter was written to the assembly in Corinth *and to all that in every place* call upon the name of the Lord. Thank God, we do call upon the name of the Lord. This statement applies to us. Do we realize that we are called into something beyond description? There is nothing higher than this: that we are all called into the fellowship of God's Son Jesus Christ.

the fellowship of God's Son Jesus Christ

What is fellowship? Fellowship is sharing in common. It is an equal, common sharing of the very nature of that which is to be shared. In other words, it is joint participation, and this is the fellowship of God's Son, Jesus Christ.

What is the fellowship of God's Son Jesus Christ? With whom is He fellowshipping? With whom does He share equally in common? With whom does He have joint participation? With fellowship, you cannot be a spectator. It is joint participation. His fellowship is with the Father in the Spirit.

A PERFECT ONENESS

He and the Father share equally, having all in common. They share everything together. He and His Father participate jointly in everything that they do. All the fullness of the Godhead dwells in Him. He is with the Father; the Father is with Him. Their fellowship is the fellowship in the Spirit. It is a perfect oneness. It is a perfect sharing together, nothing more, nothing less.

AN ETERNAL FELLOWSHIP

His fellowship with the Father and the Father's fellowship with Him are eternal. There is never a cloud, never a shadow, never a disagreement. They agree on everything. They are one in heart, one in mind, one in speech, one in work. It is so harmonious, so heavenly, and so sacred. This fellowship of God's Son Jesus Christ with the Father existed even before the foundation of the world and before there was anything created. God the Father, God the Son, and God the Holy Spirit are one, and they are in sweet fellowship. They have shared and participated together from eternity. This is the most glorious fellowship that has ever been.

EXCLUSIVE FELLOWSHIP—EXTENDED TO MANKIND

In one sense, it is the most exclusive fellowship because there are only three members—the Father, the Son, and the Holy Spirit. On the other hand, it is the most inclusive fellowship because it includes the Father, the Son, and the Holy Spirit. We cannot even imagine it because it is something way beyond us. How sweet, how perfect, how harmonious, how loving that fellowship is. There is never a break and never an interruption; it is perfect harmony.

But to our surprise, in their fellowshipping together, they came to a conclusion: because of their love, they wanted to enlarge their fellowship. They wanted to include man into their fellowship—not into their deity, the Godhead, but into their fellowship. And this was perfectly agreed upon by the Father and the Son in the Spirit. They wanted to extend it to mankind.

When God created man, He created him in His own image, after His likeness. He did not create anything else in that way—only man. Why did He do that? Was it because He already had in mind to extend His own fellowship to man that He created him in His own image? He gave man the possibility of receiving His own divine life because life is the one sole condition to be able to join that fellowship. It is a fellowship in divine life, and nothing but divine life can enter into that fellowship. So He created man in His image, which enabled him to receive His divine life. Man is the only thing created in the whole universe that can receive God's life. The angel cannot, the animal cannot, the mountain cannot, and the sea cannot. Only man was created with that capacity. If man would receive God's uncreated life, then he would be joined into the fellowship of the Father and the Son and would be able to enjoy that perfect fellowship. Divine life is the one and only condition.

THE PRICE FOR FELLOWSHIP

It was not an easy task for God to accomplish this.

The price the Father paid for fellowship

In order to bring man into His fellowship, the Father had to give up His Son:

> For God so loved the world that *he gave* his only-begotten Son (John 3:16a).

We have yet to fathom or understand what sacrifice the Father made when He gave up His only begotten Son and what love it took. This One was so one with Him that there was never a ripple. This One so pleased the Father that He could say from heaven: "This is My beloved Son in whom I have found my delight [or, am well pleased]" (Matthew 3:17b). Yet the Father gave up His only begotten Son.

The price the Son paid for fellowship

And what a price the Son paid for it! He gave up His life—not only His position on the throne, but He emptied himself of all His glory and honor. He came into this world, took on a human form in the spirit of a bondslave, and was obedient to the Father even unto death, and that the death of the cross. What a price He paid for that fellowship!

The price the Spirit pays for fellowship

And the Holy Spirit also uses all His energy with long patience to bring Christ to us. He not only begets us, but He transforms us according to the image of God's Son, Jesus Christ. What a labor of love the Holy Spirit is doing! And all this is for one reason—that the way may be opened for mankind to enter and join in that most exclusive fellowship in the universe.

The more we think about it, and the more we meditate on it, the more surprised we are. Knowing us so well, why would God do such a thing? What love is behind it! But also what responsibility!

THE APOSTLES' FELLOWSHIP

that which we have seen and heard we report to you, that ye also may have fellowship with us; and our fellowship is indeed with the Father, and with his Son Jesus Christ (I John 1:3).

The apostles shared everything that they had received from the Lord with us. They fellowshipped with us; they shared with us in common, equally, without reservation, that we may have fellowship with the apostles. What they have we have. There is a joint participation. And the apostle said, "Our fellowship is with the Father and with the Son." In other words, the apostles do not have a fellowship of their own. All the fellowship and the sharing that they give to us come from the Father and the Son.

Notice that the apostles do not have their own fellowship. As a matter of fact, the apostles reject the kind of thinking that says, "I am of Paul or I am of Apollos." No, we do not have any fellowship other than the fellowship of God's Son Jesus Christ. So the fellowship of the apostles is none other than their fellowship with the Father and with the Son. It is the same as the fellowship of God's Son, Jesus Christ.

It is said of those who believed in the Lord Jesus in the early church that

> they continued stedfastly in the apostles teaching and fellowship (Acts 2:42 KJV).

Notice that *teaching* is singular, *fellowship* is singular, and the *apostles* are plural. There are many apostles but only one teaching and only one fellowship because it is the teaching and fellowship of Christ and nothing else. That is what you find in the early church. They were all together. No one said, "This is mine." They gathered in the name of the Lord Jesus, and they talked about the Lord and nothing else.

All By Grace

We often look at I Corinthians as a very negative letter because it deals with all kinds of weakness, sin, world, flesh, unbelief, disorder, confusion, and division. How much better it would be if we only talked about Ephesians! But I Corinthians does not begin negatively; it begins with the most positive statement in the universe: "God is faithful, by whom ye have been called into the fellowship of God's Son Jesus Christ."

Do you know you have been called into this fellowship of God's Son Jesus Christ? It is not because of what you are or what I am but because of what He is. It is God's doing, and it is all grace. We have joined the most spiritual, heavenly, perfect, eternal, loving, holy fellowship in the whole universe. You and I are there, and it is all by grace.

2—Fellowship Broken

Now I exhort you, brethren, by the name of our Lord Jesus Christ, that ye all say the same thing, and that there be not among you divisions; but that ye be perfectly united in the same mind and in the same opinion. For it has been shewn to me concerning you, my brethren, by those of [the house of] Chloe, that there are strifes among you. But I speak of this, that each of you says, I am of Paul, and I of Apollos, and I of Cephas, and I of Christ. Is the Christ divided? has Paul been crucified for you? or have ye been baptised unto the name of Paul? (I Corinthians 1:10-13)

Though the church in Corinth began well in the fellowship of God's Son, gradually something happened. Paul's first letter to the Corinthians was his reply to their letter asking about a number of things that had happened. They had written a letter to Paul asking him about these problems. But strangely, in that letter they wrote to Paul, they never asked this question about the breaking of fellowship. Never! Maybe they were ashamed to ask, or maybe they were so dull that they did not even realize it was a problem. But so far as the apostle is concerned, this is the first and foremost problem because it strikes at the very center of the fellowship that we are called into. We are called into the fellowship of God's Son Jesus Christ, and when that fellowship is broken, it is the basic problem of all problems with the people of God.

So instead of answering their questions at the very start, he spent four chapters on this basic problem, and began by making a positive statement: "Don't you remember that you are called into the fellowship of God's Son Jesus Christ? Don't you remember that this is a sacred, holy, blessed calling? How can we violate our calling? This is the very center and the very life of God's calling to His people.

Division

After he had laid down that statement on their calling into fellowship (v.9), he said (v.10):

Now I exhort you, brethren,
by the name of the Lord Jesus,

What is the exhortation? The exhortation is:

that ye all say the same thing,
and that there be not among you divisions

How can we say the same thing? Are we going to tow the party line? Are we going to parrot the same word? Why is it that we cannot say the same thing?

but that ye be perfectly united
in the same mind and in the same opinion

It is because we have different minds, different opinions. If we have different minds and different opinions, how could we say the same thing?

In other words, there is something that has come in. The fellowship is the fellowship of God's Son, Jesus Christ. The fellowship is the fellowship of the Father and of the Son. The fellowship is the fellowship of life, divine life, and pure life.

But when anything comes into that fellowship that is not of God—not of Christ, not of divine life, anything that comes from the natural man, from the flesh, from the world—it breaks the very nature of that fellowship.

This is the most exclusive fellowship in the whole universe. It can only be joined by those who have divine life, and it can only be enjoyed by those who live by that divine life. If we try to bring our selves in—whether it is the good self or the bad self, anything that is not of Christ, not of God, not of the Spirit of God—then you have different minds, different opinions, and different words. These are foreign to the fellowship of God's Son, Jesus Christ. When we inject ourselves into this divine, sacred fellowship, we break it. That is division.

Saying the Same Thing

How can we say the same thing or the same word? And what is the same thing? What is the same word? Here are some examples of how the apostle Paul said the same thing:

Jesus Christ, and Him Crucified

For I did not judge it well to know anything among you save Jesus Christ, and him crucified (2:2).

Christ is Our Wisdom

But of him are ye in Christ Jesus, who has been made to us wisdom from God, and righteousness, and holiness, and redemption (1:30).

Christ is Our Power

For the word of the cross is to them that perish foolishness, but to us that are saved it is God's power (1:18).

but to those that are called, both Jews and Greeks, Christ God's power and God's wisdom (1:24).

To say the same thing is to say that "Christ is all and in all" (Colossians 3:11). That is saying the same thing, having the same mind, and the same opinion. Can it be wrong if we do that?

Is Christ Divided?

Instead of saying the same thing, they were saying different things with a divisive spirit.

each of you says

Some said, "I am of Paul. I am of Apollos. I am of Cephas. I am of Christ. Is Christ divided?" (see I Corinthians 1:12-13). In other words, when some are saying this, they are saying it with a divisive spirit. They honor the instruments of God instead of God himself.

I am of Paul

Who is Paul? He is a servant of God. He was instrumental in bringing these Corinthians to Christ. He was like a father to them. But to say, "I am of Paul. I belong to the Paul sect," divides the fellowship. It breaks up the fellowship. Whenever we have men in view instead of Christ, when we honor man more than Christ, when we center on man or follow man instead of following Christ, something is drastically wrong.

I [am] of Apollos

Some said, "I am of Apollos." Why? "Apollos is a great teacher. He taught us many doctrines and many teachings. We are for him and against Paul."

We tend to lift up one servant of God and look down upon the other instead of keeping our eyes upon the Lord and lifting up no one but Christ Jesus. That type of lifting up and looking down divides God's people.

I [am] of Cephas

Some said, "I am of Cephas [Peter]." Why? "Cephas is the first among the apostles and the most orthodox one. We are the orthodox ones, and you are not."

I [am] of Christ

Then some others, out of pride and narrowness, said: "I am of Christ. You are not of Christ; I am of Christ." To have that kind of spirit creates division.

This has been *the* problem in the church throughout the centuries. This problem is more serious than any other problem because it strikes at the very calling that God has called us into. Wherever we introduce or inject ourselves into the fellowship of God's Son Jesus Christ, this breaks it.

Though many people in Corinth rejected Paul, there were still those who lifted him up, saying, "I am of Paul." How did he react? Thank God, he used himself as an example to refute those who favored him.

Is the Christ divided?
Has Paul been crucified for you?
Or have ye been baptised unto the name of Paul?

He said: "Is Christ divided? We know nothing but Jesus Christ and Him crucified. Is Christ divided? Has Paul died for you? Are you being baptized in my name? God forbid!" Paul used himself as an example, showing the people that they needed to focus upon Christ and not upon people like Paul or Apollos or Cephas.

Who then is Apollos, and who Paul? Ministering servants, through whom ye have believed, and as the Lord has given to each. I have planted; Apollos watered; but God has given the increase. So that neither the planter is anything, nor the waterer; but God the giver of the increase (3:5-7).

Who is Paul? He is but a servant of the Lord. Who is Apollos? He is a servant of the Lord. Paul sowed, Apollos watered, but it is God who gave the increase. If you want to glory, glory in the Lord; do not glory in man.

So the apostle Paul tried to bring the mind of these Corinthian believers back to Christ. Do not think of Paul, do not think of Apollos, do not think of Cephas; think of Christ. Is He not the power of God? Is He not the wisdom of God? Everything comes from Christ, and everything returns to Christ. Other than Christ, nobody is worthy. Therefore he concluded with,

So that let no one boast in men; for all things are yours. Whether Paul, or Apollos, or Cephas, or the world, or life, or death, or things present, or things coming, all are yours; and ye are Christ's, and Christ is God's (3:21-23).

May we look away from everything and look only to Jesus, the Author and Finisher of our faith (see Hebrews 12: 2). Only by doing this can we be faithful to the fellowship that God has called us into. Just think for a moment about what price God paid to bring us into that fellowship! And to enjoy that fellowship, we also have a price to pay. We have to deny ourselves, take up the cross, and follow Him. That is the price to pay.

The reason the Corinthian believers remained carnal and had that divisive spirit is that they would not deny themselves. They did not allow the cross to work deeply in their lives, and the result was that they followed men and not Christ.

So this is an exhortation from the Lord to us. We all need to humble ourselves before the Lord and realize how sacred this fellowship is and be faithful. Thank God He is faithful, and by His grace, He is able to bring us into the full fellowship of God's Son Jesus Christ.

Dear Lord, we humble ourselves before Thee, realizing what a high calling Thou has called us to, even to share in common with Thee our Christ, our God, our Father in life. Oh, dear Lord, we pray that by Thy grace we may follow Thee, we may not in any way intrude upon that fellowship and spoil it, but we may be those who continue in the fellowship of God's Son Jesus Christ. We ask in Thy precious name. Amen.

3—Entering Into Fellowship

I Corinthians 2:1-5—And I, when I came to you, brethren, came not in excellency of word, or wisdom, announcing to you the testimony of God. For I did not judge it well to know anything among you save Jesus Christ, and him crucified. And I was with you in weakness and in fear and in much trembling; and my word and my preaching, not in persuasive words of wisdom, but in demonstration of the Spirit and of power; that your faith might not stand in men's wisdom, but in God's power.

We often think of this first letter to the Corinthians as very negative. There are many things covered that we do not like even to mention but thank God when you actually look into the letter, you find that it begins with a most positive note:

God is faithful by whom ye have been called into the fellowship of His Son Jesus Christ our Lord (1:9).

Man may be unfaithful, but God is always faithful. He is always faithful to himself, to His own word, to His own promise, and to His calling.

We are told that God has called us—even people like us who are like the Corinthians—into something which is tremendously glorious. I do not have the words to describe it, but if you truly meditate on it, you will be amazed at what a calling God has called us to. He has called us into the fellowship, into sharing in common, into participating in the fellowship of God's Son, Jesus Christ our Lord.

The fellowship of God's Son, Jesus Christ, is with the Father. So in I John, it says, "Our fellowship is with the Father and with the Son, and now this fellowship between the Father and the Son, this sharing together, this participating together of the Father and of the Son in the Spirit, is now being extended to us." He has called us into His own fellowship. This is a tremendous statement.

This is an "on-high calling" (Philippians 3:14), a "holy calling" (II Timothy 1:9 ASV), a "heavenly calling" (Hebrews 3:1), and we are all called into it. This calling measures everything in our lives, personally and corporately. The apostle Paul spends the first four chapters of I Corinthians on this matter.

Christ and Him Crucified

As we continue with chapter 2, it explains to us how we come into this fellowship. The apostle Paul says,

And I, when I came to you, brethren,
came not in excellency of word, or wisdom,
announcing to you the testimony of God.

He went to Corinth to announce the testimony of God, but before he went, he made a judgment. It was not something careless or casual, but he actually deliberated and determined it before the Lord.

The judgment he made was that when he went to Corinth, he would know nothing among them but Jesus Christ and Him crucified.

For I did not judge it well
to know anything among you
save Jesus Christ, and him crucified.

Why did he make such a judgment? We know the Corinthians were noted for their intelligence and their eloquence. There is a proverb that says, "You *speak* like a Corinthian," and it means that you are very eloquent. At the same time, another proverbial saying says, "You *live* like a Corinthian." That is to say that you live a morally corrupt life. In other words, the Corinthians could talk beautifully, but they lived an ugly life.

Therefore, before Paul went into their midst, he made this decision. He knew what he was doing. He said, "When I come to you, I will know nothing but Jesus Christ and Him crucified." That was the one and only thing that could deliver them.

This is the testimony of God. If you want to know what the testimony of God is or what it is that God testifies to us, it is Jesus Christ and Him crucified: "This is My beloved Son in whom I am well pleased." This is the gospel; this is the testimony of God—Jesus. "His name shall be called Jesus because He shall deliver His people from their sins" (see Matthew 1:21). He is Christ because He is the anointed One, the One sent by the Father on a mission to save the lost, to redeem the sick, and He is our Lord.

The Son of God came into this world to deliver the Corinthians from their corrupt lives and turn them into saints of God. This is the same thing He does with us. It is all Jesus Christ and Him crucified.

Why is it also "him crucified"? If our Lord Jesus had come into this world and fully, beautifully, totally represented what God is or what man should be, that would not save us. His life is so perfect that it actually would condemn us instead of justifying us. How is it that when He came into this world and lived such a perfect life, He was able to save us sinners? How did He do it? It is through His crucifixion.

The cross is a symbol of shame, of curse, and of death. We do not worship the cross itself; we worship Him who was crucified on the cross. It is because our Lord Jesus, who knew no sin was made sin for us, that we might become God's righteousness in Him (see II Corinthians 5:21). This is salvation. This is the testimony of God.

To put it another way, God has called us into the fellowship of His Son Jesus Christ. Now, how are we going to join that fellowship? We mentioned before that the fellowship between the Father and the Son is a fellowship in divine life. It is a fellowship in the Spirit. It is a perfect, harmonious, beautiful, heavenly, spiritual fellowship. So the only condition for anyone to join the fellowship of God's Son Jesus Christ is through life. It is not our natural life, nor created life, nor Adamic life, nor fallen life; it is by His divine life. It is a fellowship of life; it is a fellowship in life.

How are we going to receive divine life, God's life, so that we may be able to join that heavenly fellowship? The only way we can have life is through the finished work of Christ on the cross, where He released His life. Through the cross, not only have our sins been forgiven, but the life that was released through death and resurrection has been given to all who believe. That is the way we come into life.

What is eternal life? In John 17:3, we are told, "And this is the eternal life, that they should know Thee, the only true God, and Jesus Christ whom thou hast sent." Eternal life is a living, experiential knowledge of God and the Lord Jesus Christ—"In him was life, and the life was the light of men" (John 1:4).

How do we answer God's calling? What is the way that we can join in that fellowship? It is not a man-made way. No matter how man tries, man will never be able to enter in that divine fellowship of the Father and the Son in the Spirit. God has provided the way for us to enter into that fellowship. And by the grace of God, all who believe what He has done for us through Jesus Christ and Him crucified—not because of what we are—is why we are all in that one fellowship, that divine fellowship, that holy, spiritual, heavenly fellowship.

Remember one thing. Our fellowship can never rise above our life, the kind of life we have, the kind of sharing we have. If the life that one has is a sinful, selfish, corrupt natural life, then our sharing with one another will also be earthly, worldly, sinful, and corrupt. But if the life that we receive is a divine life, then it delivers us out of that which is earthly and puts us into that which is heavenly. In other words, it is His life that not only brings us into the fellowship of God's Son Jesus Christ, but it is the same life that enables us to fellowship on a higher ground. That is how important life is.

The apostle Paul made the right decision when he said, "I know nothing among you but Jesus Christ and Him crucified." And if the Corinthian believers had really accepted all that was involved in Jesus Christ and Him crucified, they would truly have been in that fellowship of God's Son Jesus Christ, and their spiritual condition would have been different from what you read in the letter Paul wrote to them. But unfortunately, their receiving of Jesus Christ and Him crucified was rather incomplete. In other words, they received the finished work of our Lord Jesus on the cross for their sins. They came to Him and accepted Him as their Savior—and they were saved—but they did not receive the Lord Jesus as their life. They did not allow the life of the Lord Jesus to rule over them, so they still lived in their own natural life. The world, self, even sin had such power over them that they continued to live on the lower plane; therefore, their fellowship with one another was on a lower plane. That is the way they treated one another and shared with one another. They could not rise above to that which is heavenly and spiritual.

Or, to put it another way—they received Jesus Christ and Him crucified in an objective way. In other words, what Christ had done for them on the cross they received, but it was for them, so that their sins would be forgiven. As a result, they were still self-centered and lived for themselves. They had not received Jesus Christ and Him crucified into their very being and allowed the cross to work subjectively in their lives. So even though they had eternal life, they still lived by their natural life, and that was the way of the church in Corinth. They could not rise above the life they possessed.

It was different with the apostle Paul. He illustrated it this way: "For I did not judge it well to know anything among you save Jesus Christ, and him crucified. And I was with you in weakness and in fear and in much trembling" (I Corinthians 2:2-3).

When you read these two verses, I wonder if you feel there is a contradiction. He came into the midst of the

Corinthians announcing to them the testimony of God, which was Jesus Christ and Him crucified. There is nothing more wonderful, more powerful, or more glorious than Jesus Christ and Him crucified. It is such a glorious gospel. Now it is true that in II Corinthians 13, we are told that Jesus was crucified in weakness, but He lives by the power of God (v. 4. When our Lord Jesus was crucified, it appears to be weakness, and yet before He passed away, He shouted, "It is finished!" It is a shout of victory. In other words, the testimony that God gives—Jesus Christ and Him crucified—is a strong, glorious, powerful announcement, yet the messenger was weak, fearful, and trembling. That is a contradiction.

Some people think that before the apostle Paul went to Corinth, he had traveled through places like Galatia and other places that were full of malaria, and he had caught it. And when you have malaria, and an attack comes, you tremble. So he said, "I am in much trembling and fear and weak." Malaria makes you very weak, and it can affect your eyesight. That is the reason Paul said, "Look at what large letters I write." His eye sight was so poor that some people say when he arrived at Corinth, he was physically down. And that is the reason why he said, "I am in much trembling and fear and weakness."

However, I believe there is more to it than that. When Paul went to Corinth, he preached the gospel, announcing the testimony of God, and many turned to the Lord. But the Bible says that Paul was afraid, and God had to appear to him in a vision or a dream, and say, "Fear not. Do not stop speaking; do not be silent. I have many people in this city" (see Acts 18: 9- 10). So we believe that the fear, the trembling, and the weakness that the apostle Paul felt at that time was more than physical. There is a spiritual context to it. He was really afraid for his life, and that is why he was trembling and very weak.

Then he said, "My word and my preaching, not in persuasive words of wisdom, but in demonstration of the Spirit and of power" (I Corinthians 2:4).

Paul was naturally eloquent because as a Pharisee he was trained to speak and to argue. In Acts 17, when he was speaking in Athens, how eloquent he was. He could match the Corinthians with eloquence and with his intelligence, but he determined, and then made a judgment, that he would not speak in persuasive words of wisdom. He would not speak beautifully. He would not try to match intelligence or eloquence with the Corinthians. He would rather let the cross work in his life and deliver him from what he would like to say beautifully, logically, and powerfully. He would give up himself and just trust the Lord and the Holy Spirit to demonstrate God's power. In other words, he not only preached Jesus Christ and Him crucified, He also allowed this to so work in his life that he was a crucified messenger of the crucified message. Paul, as a person, was himself crucified, and Christ became his life. Even in announcing the testimony of God it was not in man's wisdom but in God's power. It is all of God and none of Paul.

Jesus Christ and Him crucified is not only an objective truth but it is a subjective experience. It is not only that Jesus Christ was crucified on Calvary but that cross had entered into the very life of Paul, putting him to death and allowing the life of Christ to take charge, so that everything that came out of Paul was Christ—and not Paul. That is fellowship. And that kind of fellowship is powerful because it brings life to people. So we can see from this what the Corinthians lacked. They had received Jesus Christ and Him crucified in an objective way, and they were benefited because they were saved. They did receive life, but that life was not able to take charge over them because they were still living by their old life. That is why their fellowship was in a low state.

Jesus Christ and Him crucified is not only the way that leads us into *the* fellowship but it is also the way for our fellowshipping. If we want to enjoy the fellowship of God's Son Jesus Christ, we cannot enjoy it if we still live by our self-life. We have to allow the cross to work deeply in each one of us, and then, out of His life there will be that heavenly, spiritual, glorious fellowship.

Again, I would like to emphasize that our fellowship cannot rise above what our life is. Our life determines the kind of fellowship we have. Therefore, if we really live by the life of Christ daily and allow Christ to be our life, then our joy may be full. In I John 1 the apostle John said, "We are having fellowship with you. We are sharing Christ and God the Father with you because this is who our fellowship is with. And if you too will share the Father and the Son, the result will be that our joy will be full." There is nothing that gives you more joy among God's people more than when you really have the fellowship of God's Son Jesus Christ. The reason we are not filled with joy is because we fellowship ourselves. But if we will only fellowship with Christ and with one another with His life, what He means to us, what He has revealed to us, what He has done in our lives then we will all grow in grace, we will grow in the life of Christ, and there will be much joy.

Wisdom

But we speak wisdom among the perfect; but wisdom not of this world, nor of the rulers of this world, who come to nought. But we speak God's wisdom in a mystery, that hidden wisdom which God had predetermined before the ages for our glory: which none of the princes of this age knew, (for had they known, they would not have crucified the Lord of glory;) but according as it is written, Things which eye has not seen, and ear not heard, and which have not come into man's heart, which God has prepared for them that love him, but God has revealed to us by his Spirit; for the Spirit searches all things, even the depths of God. For who of men hath known the things of a man except the spirit of the man which is in him? thus also the things of God knows no one except the Spirit of God. But we have received, not the spirit of the world, but the Spirit which is of God, that we may know the things which have been freely given to us of God: which also we speak, not in words taught by human wisdom, but in those taught by the Spirit, communicating spiritual things by spiritual means. But the natural man does not receive the things of the Spirit of God, for they are folly to him; and he cannot know them because they are spiritually discerned; but the spiritual discerns all things, and he is discerned of no one. For who has known the mind of the Lord, who shall instruct him? But we have the mind of Christ (I Corinthians 2:6-16).

When Paul came into their midst, he said he made a judgment to know nothing among them except Jesus Christ and Him crucified. Was that all? No, he also said,

But we speak wisdom among the perfect

There are two words to notice here.

Wisdom

The first word is wisdom. In chapter 1, Paul has already said that the Greeks seek wisdom and the Jews seek power. But Paul said, "We preach Christ crucified." To the Jews, it is weakness; to the Greeks, it is foolishness, but Jesus Christ is the power of God and the wisdom of God. So there are two kinds of wisdom. There is one wisdom which is the wisdom of this world, and the wisdom of this world crucified the Lord. It is the wisdom from beneath; it is carnal, worldly and even devilish. But there is a wisdom which is from above, and here Paul says, "We will talk about that wisdom." There is a wisdom, but it is a different kind of wisdom; it is God's wisdom in a mystery.

Perfect

The other word to notice is *perfect*. He said, "Among the perfect we also speak wisdom." Who are "the perfect"? The word *perfect* in the Scripture does not mean sinless perfect because there is only one man—Jesus Christ—in the whole world that is sinlessly perfect. But the word *perfect* in the Scripture is used in such a way as to mean grown-up, matured, or those who are "no longer babes." With the babes in Christ, all you can talk about is Jesus Christ and Him crucified. That is the foundation, but in that foundation, there is a wisdom.

But you do not talk about wisdom until God's people are growing up. And how do they grow up? They grow up through fellowship. We grow up spiritually by our fellowshipping with Christ and with God. And we grow up together by our fellowshipping together in Christ and with Christ. And if we are growing up, then God will open our eyes to see His wisdom.

God's Wisdom Predetermined

The apostle Paul described God's wisdom in mystery, saying that it is a hidden mystery and a hidden wisdom. This is the wisdom of God; it is hidden even before the ages, even before God created anything. In eternity past there was a wisdom of God. He said in verse 7: "But we speak God's wisdom in a mystery, that hidden wisdom which God had predetermined before the ages for our glory."

Think of that! The wisdom of God in a mystery is something that God had predetermined before the ages, even before He created anything. God had already determined one thing, and that thing is for our glory.

Oftentimes we think if only we can be saved out of hell and into heaven that will be glorious. But God said, "That is nothing. What I have prepared for you for glory is something that is really glorious, as glorious as God. Can you imagine that? That is God's wisdom.

God's Wisdom Prepared

It is not only predetermined but it is also something prepared: "Things which eye has not seen, and ear not heard, and which have not come into man's heart, which God has prepared for them that love him" (I Corinthians 2:9).

It is something that eye has never seen, ear has never heard, and it has never even entered into man's heart. Nobody has ever thought of it. Confucius never thought of it, nor did Socrates think of it. No man has ever thought of it because it is beyond man's imagination. It is something that God not only predetermined but also prepared. Think of that! Predetermined means that He decided to do something, but it is more than that. He also prepared for it for those who love Him. He already has in His mind that glorious thing for those who are constrained by His love and love Him as He loves them.

God's Wisdom Revealed by the Spirit

This is something in the heart of God and mind of God. Nobody knows. It is a mystery. How can this secret be known? Is it by searching? No, it is beyond our intelligence. It is revealed by the Spirit of God. Think of that! It is predetermined, prepared, and now it is being revealed. God makes it known to us by His Spirit.

In Ephesians 3, the apostle Paul said, "I know the mystery of the Christ." This mystery has been hidden through the ages but now has been revealed to the prophets and the apostles. It has been opened up and is now an open secret. Do you know it? You can because it has been revealed.

God's Wisdom Freely Given

"That we may know the things that have been freely given to us of God" (I Corinthians 2:12b). It is not only revealed, but it is to be freely given to us. You do not need to pay anything because it is freely given to you. Who has the mind of God? But we have the mind of Christ. In other words, what God has predetermined before the ages, and what He has prepared for those who love Him, has now been revealed. We now have the mind of Christ; therefore, we know it.

The Church

Do you know what it is? Of course, it is the church. Paul was not able to come out openly and say, "I am going to share with you the mystery of the Christ which is the church," as he did in Ephesians. He could not say that because they were still babes and could not understand. They may even have misunderstood with such questions as this: "What is the church about? Why is it so important? Isn't our personal life, our family life, or our social life more important than the church? What is the church?" Surely if you grow in the Lord, you grow into this mystery.

How can we grow into it? It is by fellowship. When you are truly fellowshipping in Christ Jesus, sharing with one another the Christ you know, the Father you know, not only will you be filled with joy, but your understanding will be opened, and you will see that God's purpose is more than personal—it is the body; it is the church. That is what fellowship is.

Unfortunately, today we come to know what we call the church by hearing the truth about it. Now there is nothing wrong with the truth. Therefore, in our mind we all know what the church is. Hopefully we all know that the church is a physical building. "I go to church." Where do you go to church? Where is the church? Is it a building like this? Is this the church? No, this is where the church meets, but it is not the church. I hope we all know the truth that the church is the body of Christ, the called-out ones gathered together under the name of the Lord Jesus with His presence there.

Strictly speaking, fellowship is just another word for the church. It is the active word for the church because when you speak of the church you think more of the truth. When you talk about fellowship, you think more of experience; but it is one and the same thing. If you love the church, you love fellowship. If you live a life just by yourself and think that this is all you need, you do not know what you are missing.

So here in this second chapter, the apostle Paul is trying to show the Corinthian believers how glorious it is when we enter into the fellowship of God's Son Jesus Christ instead of fellowshipping about who we are or what we have done with one another which would be disastrous, or even fellowshipping what we have heard—and not first-hand experience. If brothers and sisters truly realize that they are called into the fellowship of God's Son Jesus Christ and are willing to accept the cross working in their lives to take away self and allow Christ to be *the* fellowship, and thus fellowship with nothing but Christ, what joy it will be, what enlightenment it will be. Our eyes will be opened, and we will begin to realize it is the church, and we will be brought into the reality of the eternal purpose of God.

Sometimes I think the way we come to the church is probably from the truth side instead of the experience side. And if we come to the church through the truth side, probably sadness and not joy will fill our hearts. But if we come to the church from the experiential side or from the fellowshipping side, we will be filled with joy. So may the Lord help us.

Dear Lord, how we praise and thank Thee for being so kind, so gracious to us in extending Thy own fellowship with the Father to us. And Lord, do forgive us for not knowing how glorious that fellowship is. We pray that Thou will deliver us from fellowshipping on the lower ground. But Lord, we pray that Thou will do such a work in our lives that Christ may be shared one with another, that we may grow up spiritually and see the beauty, the glory of the church, the body of Christ, the bride of the Lamb. And we give You glory. In Thy precious name we pray. Amen.

4—How He Builds

I Corinthians 3:10-17—According to the grace of God which has been given to me, as a wise architect [foreman], I have laid the foundation, but another builds upon it. But let each see how he builds upon it. For other foundation can no man lay besides that which is laid, which is Jesus Christ. Now if any one build upon this foundation, gold, silver, precious stones, wood, grass, straw, the work of each shall be made manifest; for the day shall declare it, because it is revealed in fire; and the fire shall try the work of each what it is. If the work of any one which he has built upon the foundation shall abide, he shall receive a reward. If the work of any one shall be consumed, he shall suffer loss, but he shall be saved, but so as through the fire. Do ye not know that ye are the temple of God, and that the Spirit of God dwells in you? If any one corrupt the temple of God, him shall God destroy, for the temple of God is holy, and such are ye.

We are still in I Corinthians chapters 1-4. The number one problem with the church in Corinth was their division, but Paul approaches this problem in a positive way. Why is division so serious? It is because there is a calling that we who believe in the Lord Jesus have been called into. And if we only can see our calling it will deliver us not only from division but from all the other things that you find being dealt with in this letter.

We need to remember a glorious fact, and it is that all of us who believe in the Lord Jesus have been called into the fellowship of God's Son Jesus Christ. We are to share in common with Him. We are to share the Lord Jesus Christ with one another. We are in such a fellowship, and because this fellowship is so holy, so heavenly, so spiritual, and so in life, therefore anything that is not holy, heavenly, spiritual or in life will be a contradiction to that fellowship.

The fellowship of the Lord Jesus, the Son of God, is with the Father, and His Father fellowships with Him. In that fellowship there is no darkness, no unrighteousness and nothing unlovely. It is a perfect and harmonious fellowship. It is a fellowship that is selfless and shares everything. It withholds nothing. Whatever the Father has, He gives to His Son. Whatever the Son has, He gives back to the Father. Their fellowship is in the Holy Spirit, and now this fellowship has been extended to us who believe in Him. The Lord Jesus shares His Father with us and does not withhold anything that He knows is of His Father. In like manner, the Father shares His Son with us and does not withhold anything that He has given to His Son. And this is how we are called into fellowship with one another.

We have mentioned that we enter into this fellowship by believing in Jesus Christ and Him crucified, and the way we fellowship with one another is also based upon the same thing. To put it simply, when we fellowship and we share with one another, what do we share? Do we share ourselves with one another? No; we share the Christ we know with one another. And in order to share Christ with one another, we have to allow His cross to work in our lives, so that we may know Christ as our life—not only as our Savior but as our life. In this way we learn to live by that life.

Calling Involves Responsibility

Chapters 3-4 are still on fellowship, but it tells us that in that fellowship there is something going on. Calling involves responsibility. We are called into the fellowship of God's Son Jesus Christ, and because we have been called into such a privilege, there is a responsibility that comes upon each and every one of us. The Bible says that many are called, but few are chosen. In other words, we are all called into that fellowship, but whether we bear that responsibility and fulfill it is something to be determined. Fellowship is not an empty word. It is not just a theological thought. Fellowship is living, and it is very real. It touches our life—not only our personal life but our family life, our social life and our church life. In other words, fellowship touches our whole being, and because of that, there is something that comes out of fellowship. Fellowship has to do with building, and that is the reason why in chapter 3 the apostle Paul mentions this.

Fellowshipping is Building

How is the church built? How is the temple of God built? It is built by the fellowshipping of God's children. As we fellowship we build. We either build or we destroy. There is a responsibility in us. The Lord Jesus said, "On this rock I will build My church, and Hades gates shall not prevail against it." He shared with us what He is and all that He has done for us. He is the foundation, and upon that foundation He said, "I will build My church."

What is His church? His church is nothing but God's building, the temple of God, that in which God dwells by His Spirit. He is the foundation, and we who are called into that fellowship are building upon that foundation. The apostle Paul said that he was a wise foreman. He was not the architect because that is Christ himself. He was a wise foreman because he laid the only foundation that could be laid. Not only Paul but all the apostles laid the foundation as it says in Ephesians 2:20: "The household of God, being built upon the foundation of the apostles and prophets." What does that mean? It means that the apostles reported to us that which they had seen and heard, contemplated, understood, experienced, what they touched of that word of life, that eternal life, which is Christ Jesus. And they faithfully shared with us all that they learned of Christ. That is laying the foundation.

However, it is not only Paul or Apollos or the other apostles that are doing such work; we all are called to have a part in that building. That is the reason Paul said, "I am as a wise foreman. I have laid the foundation among you Corinthians, and that foundation can be nothing else but Jesus Christ. Let each see how he builds upon it." He wants every one of us to see, to understand, to know, to take it to heart, how each of us builds on it.

We discover that fellowshipping is building. As we fellowship with the Father and with the Son we are building something into our life, and as we fellowship with our brothers and sisters we are building something into our brothers and sisters. We are all involved in the building of the house of God, of that holy temple of God, of that place where God is to dwell in His Spirit.

After you are saved, you are immediately put into that building work. Whether you are conscious of it or not, it does not matter. Even if you are not aware of it, you are building something—whether you are alone, when you are with your brothers and sisters, in the family, or even when you are at work. You have been called into that fellowship, therefore consciously or unconsciously, continuously, day and night, you are doing some building work. And this is not an ordinary building. It is building the house of God, the temple of God, the dwelling place of God, the church. I hope this will be deeply impressed upon every one of us.

Oftentimes, we forget that we are building something. We think that it does not matter, that when we are alone nothing happens. But even when you are by yourself, some building is going on. Whether you are with brothers and sisters or alone, consciously or unconsciously, you are building something into that house. The foundation is Christ. In other words, what is built upon that foundation has to be of the same quality, the same nature, the same character as the foundation.

The Church is the Extension of Christ

What is the church? The church is the extension of Christ. That is the reason in I Corinthians 12 it says, "The body is one but has many members. There are many members but one body, so also is the Christ." That which is built upon that foundation, if it is going to be God's dwelling place, has to be of the same nature, quality, and character as the foundation which is Jesus Christ.

What are you building into it? You build Jesus Christ upon that foundation. That is the extension of the foundation. So the Bible says that our Lord Jesus is not only the foundation, He is also the cornerstone; He is not only the cornerstone, He is also the top stone. In other words, the whole building is a corporate expression of the foundation of what He is. And if that is the case, then how important it is and how careful we must be as to how we build. We are all building. You may not feel it, but it is going on. And do not forget that you are building something of eternal value.

Our God created the heavens and earth and all the things in heaven and on earth and even underneath the earth all by himself. He did not ask your help. But strangely, when He is building His own house in which to dwell, He calls all of us to join Him in that work. It is marvelous in our eyes. What faith He has put on us! He knows what we are. He knows what we will be doing, and yet He has faith in us. He called us into fellowship, and by fellowshipping we build His house. Do not think that you are engaged in this building only when you come to the meetings. Even if you are in your home by yourself, you are contributing something to it, good or bad, twenty-four hours a day. There is no vacation because the work is urgent.

So the apostle Paul says, "But let each see how he builds upon it." If you are not the Lord's, if you are not saved, if you do not believe in the Lord Jesus, then you are not in that building work. But once you believe in the Lord Jesus, you have been called whether you like it or not, and the responsibility is upon you whether you are conscious of it or not. So let us be careful as to how we build on it.

The Material for the House

Gold-Silver-Precious Stones

We discover that the emphasis seems to be on the material because Paul says, "Some may build with gold, silver, precious stones, and others may build with wood, grass, straw." So basically, there are two kinds of building. How do you build? You can build either with gold, silver, and precious stones, or you can build with wood, grass, and straw. We know that gold in the Scriptures always represents the nature of God because gold is the most precious metal, incorruptible, weighty, of value, shiny, lasting. So in the Bible we find that gold always represents something of God. The holiest of all was overlaid with pure gold. The ark was overlaid inside and outside with gold. The mercy seat was pure gold, and even the lampstand was pure gold—all representing the nature of God.

In the Scriptures, silver represents the redemption of our Lord Jesus because we find in Exodus 30 that every Israelite, who was numbered above twenty years of age, had to pay ransom money of half a shekel. Therefore, silver represents the redemption of our Lord Jesus who gave His own life as a ransom for us.

Precious stones speak of the work of the Holy Spirit because these matters have to go through pressure, heat, darkness, and time, until they become precious stones. How patiently the Holy Spirit in the dark, as it were, secretly works in our lives in order that precious stones may be produced. So the gold, silver, and precious stones all represent what is of God, Christ, and the Holy Spirit, and you can build into that house with such material. Of course, if you want to build with such materials it will cost you something. Gold is costly; silver is costly, and precious stones are costly. These things are not free. You will have to pay a cost for them, and the cost that you have to pay is yourself. Self is the cost. You have to deny self, take up the cross, and follow the Lord. That is the ultimate cost, and that is the way the nature of God is incorporated into our lives and the finished work of Christ becomes a reality in us. The Holy Spirit is able to constitute Christ into our lives, and out of that which you have received you share with your brothers and sisters. That is building with gold, silver, and precious stones.

Furthermore, if you build with gold, silver, and precious stones, you cannot build a huge building with it because they are so costly. It may be small, little, hardly seen, but it is there, it is real, and it is permanent.

Wood-Grass-Straw

On the other hand, you may build with wood, grass and straw. Wood in the Scripture always speaks of man. Men are like trees. You remember in Judges 9, Jotham used a parable about the trees. The trees wanted to find a king, and they said to the fig tree and to the vine, "Be our king." And they said, "No; we have our responsibility. We produce wine, we produce fatness for God. We do not want to be king." So they asked the thorn bush, and the thorn bush said, "Okay, if you want me to be king, come under me, otherwise fire will come and burn you up." So tree always represents the nature of man.

What is grass? In I Peter 1 we are told that all flesh is as grass and its beauty as flowers. So grass represents the glory of man. It is fading, withering.

Then there is straw. I think we all remember how Pharaoh commanded the children of Israel to make bricks with straw. So straw is the work of man. In other words, it is everything that comes out of man, of yourself, of your natural self. There is no working of the cross in that life. So what you put in is yourself, and because wood, grass, and straw are cheap you do not need to pay a great cost. You can build a huge building with it, and everybody can see it. Is it theory? No; Paul illustrates this.

Fleshy or Fleshly

At the beginning of chapter 3 Paul tells us how the Corinthians built into that building in their fellowship. He said, "I, brethren, have not been able to speak to you as to spiritual, but as to fleshly; as to babes in Christ." I would like to change the word *fleshly, sarkikos,* to *fleshy,* to better distinguish it. Now a babe is very fleshy. A babe attracts people. Everybody considers a babe attractive because he is very fleshy; he does not hide anything. That is what he is. If he wants to cry, he cries. It does not matter who is around him. If he is hungry he wants to eat; he is very fleshy. Now when we are babes in Christ, that is what we are—lovely but fleshy. And those who are babes in Christ can only drink milk. What is milk? Milk is predigested food. Your mother has predigested the food and then it becomes milk for the babe. In other words, you have not exercised your spiritual faculties to distinguish good or evil, so you need something that has already been ready-made for you, and that is a babe. So babes in Christ have to be fed with milk. People have to digest God's word and then it becomes a message, and it is delivered to you as milk so that it is easy to digest. You do not need to exercise yourself. That is a babe.

What is the situation of babes? He said, "There are among you emulation and strife, are ye not carnal, *[sarkikos]*?" Carnal does not only mean "the composition of the matter." Now we are composed of flesh and this is the material, this is the matter; so it is fleshly, but it is neutral. In other words, there is no evil, moral sense within it, but when it says "fleshly or carnal" there is a moral element injected in it. So we all begin as babes, but we have to outgrow babyhood. If you do not outgrow your babyhood, then you become carnal; you become fleshly—not fleshy but fleshly because there is a moral sense behind it. And when you are fleshly, the symptoms are emulation, jealousy, envy, strife, quarreling. This is acting according to man. Even if you are a Christian you will act according to the man of the world. There is no difference in outward actions. These are babes in Christ; they do not grow up.

The Cross Enables Us to Grow Up

Why didn't the Corinthian believers grow up? They refused to accept the cross of Christ into their lives. They wanted to remain as they were—to be themselves. What is wrong with that? It is *my* opinion, *my* thought, *my* way; this is how I see it; this is what I want. They were babes in Christ. That is wood, grass, and straw, and that is the way you build into it.

On the other hand, the apostle Paul used himself and Apollos as the opposite example. So in chapter 4:1 the apostle Paul says, "Let a man so account of us as servants of Christ, and stewards of the mysteries of God." Paul is saying, "We are servants; we are nobodies. Don't uplift us; uplift Christ. We are but servants. It does not matter what people think about us, the one who examines us is the Lord."

As you read chapter 4 you find that he is building into this house through fellowship. He said, "To the present hour we both hunger and thirst, and are in nakedness, and buffeted, and wander without a home, and labour, working with our own hands. Railed at, we bless; persecuted, we suffer it; insulted, we entreat; we are become as the offscouring of the world, the refuse of all, until now" (vv. 11-13). This is building with gold, silver, and precious stones.

In building with their own flesh the Corinthians thought they were filled, they were enriched, they were reigning, they had become strong and they were in glory. But Paul and the apostles, in building with gold, silver, and precious stones, were appointed to death. They had become a spectacle to the world, both to angels and man, fools for Christ's sake. Isn't it true that people who build with wood, grass, and straw can build such a huge building? Everybody can see it and praise it. And yet if you build with gold, silver, and precious stones it can hardly be seen. People will think you are doing nothing, accomplishing nothing. Isn't it true? But the problem is if these remain as they are forever, then why be foolish? Why be wise in the eyes of man? But unfortunately it says, "The work of each shall be made manifest; for the day shall declare it, because it is revealed in fire; and the fire shall try the work of each what it is" (v. 13).

The Judgment Seat of Christ

One day we shall all appear at the judgment seat of Christ. Now some people may not know this. They say, "If I believe in the Lord Jesus, isn't it true that I will not be judged anymore because Christ has been judged for me on Calvary's cross?" That is true. If you believe in the Lord Jesus, Christ has already been judged for you; therefore the judgment has passed over you, and you are saved. But remember, that is the judgment of the great white throne. It does not mean that a believer will not be judged. The believer will have another kind of judgment. It is called the judgment seat of Christ.

II Corinthians 5:10 says that we shall all be manifested before the judgment seat of Christ, and what we have done in the body shall be reckoned with. Romans 14:10 says we shall all appear or stand before the judgment seat of God. In other words, there is a judgment that we as believers will go through. We will not go through the judgment of the great white throne because throne speaks of government. There, eternal death or eternal life is to be decided. Thank God that judgment has passed over us because Christ was judged for us and God is righteous. He cannot judge us again because He has already judged our substitute, Christ. Thank God for that. But that does not mean because you are a child of God there will be no judgment at all. There will be a family judgment. As the family of God we shall all one day appear before the judgment seat of Christ. When will that be? Where will it be? The Bible tells us at the last hour, when the trumpet shall sound, those who are dead in Christ will be raised from the dead, and those who are living and remain will all be caught up to the air where the Lord is with the overcomers. We shall

all be gathered before the judgment seat of Christ and everyone will be judged accordingly.

We are called into the fellowship of God's Son Jesus Christ, and therefore we are all engaged in that building. One day, what we have put in will be judged, even by fire. Isn't that strange? If it is judged by something else, the wood, the grass, the straw may stand, but if it is by fire then all that is of wood, grass, or straw will be burned. However, all that is of gold, silver, and precious stones will shine. The fire will try each work.

God is a Consuming Fire

What is the fire? In Hebrews 12 we are told that our God is a consuming fire. He is the fire. He is to examine us according to what He is. To put it another way, at the judgment seat of Christ, what Christ is looking for is himself. What have you put into your fellowshipping? Do you put in Christ or are you putting in something else? Something else will be burned but Christ will be glorified. Now that is the difference. Yet the Bible makes it very clear to us, that if we build with gold, silver, and precious stones and they stand and go through the fire, we shall receive a reward. This is not gift but reward. And we know the reward is the kingdom to come. You shall reign with Christ for a thousand years. But if the work of anyone shall be consumed by the fire, what will happen? He will suffer loss because his whole life is lost after he was saved— nothing counts before God. But he shall be saved, only as through fire, barely saved. That has nothing to do with eternal salvation, but it is a matter of losing the kingdom.

This is a serious thing. Sometimes we take our Christian life carelessly, thinking that it does not matter what I am doing, or it does not matter what I am not doing. It does not matter how I live or how I do not live. It does not matter when I am alone or when I am meeting with brothers and sisters. Oftentimes we come to the meeting without contributing. But if we do not contribute, it is contributing something to that building process. Something is still going on. Are you building or destroying?

"Do ye not know that ye are the temple of God, and that the Spirit of God dwells in you?" (v. 16). We are the temple of God collectively, and the Holy Spirit dwells in us. "If any one corrupt the temple of God, him shall God destroy" (v. 17a). The word *corrupt* and *destroy* are the same words in Greek. We can corrupt the temple by putting in wood, grass, straw, or we can build the temple by putting in gold, silver, and precious stones. What are we putting in? You may think you are not putting in anything. But when you are not putting in anything, you are putting in wood, grass, and straw because that process is going on day and night unceasingly. Even when you are alone it matters.

"For the temple of God is holy and such are ye" (v. 17b). Thank God for that. So let us be warned and let us be encouraged. This is the reason why we, who are called into the fellowship of God's Son Jesus Christ, must be true to our calling and be responsible.

5—Leaven and Judgment

I Corinthians 5:1-8—It is universally reported that there is fornication among you, and such fornication as is not even among the nations, so that one should have his father's wife. And ye are puffed up, and ye have not rather mourned, in order that he that has done this deed might be taken away out of the midst of you. For I, as absent in body but present in spirit, have already judged as present, to deliver, in the name of our Lord Jesus Christ (ye and my spirit being gathered together, with the power of our Lord Jesus Christ), him that has so wrought this: to deliver him, I say, being such, to Satan for destruction of the flesh, that the spirit may be saved in the day of the Lord Jesus. Your boasting is not good. Do ye not know that a little leaven leavens the whole lump? Purge out the old leaven, that ye may be a new lump, according as ye are unleavened. For also our passover, Christ, has been sacrificed; so that let us celebrate the feast, not with old leaven, nor with leaven of malice and wickedness, but with unleavened bread of sincerity and truth.

We have been fellowshipping together on this most important subject—our calling. As the redeemed of the Lord we have been called into a wonderful fellowship, the fellowship of God's Son Jesus Christ. Could you ever imagine that people such as we are called by God in His great love toward us into the fellowship of His Son Jesus Christ? Think of the fellowship of God's Son Jesus Christ. He is fellowshipping and sharing together without any reservation in perfect harmony with His Father in the Spirit. And likewise, the Father opened himself completely to the Son, withholding nothing from Him, sharing everything together with His beloved Son. And just think that God has opened up this divine, holy, perfect, eternal fellowship to us who are redeemed, and this is the privilege we have been called to. Every one of us, who are redeemed of the Lord, has been called; therefore we ought to know nothing save Jesus Christ and Him crucified.

The apostle Paul said, "I come among you Corinthians, and I have determined to know nothing among you save Jesus Christ and Him crucified." It is Jesus Christ and Him crucified that brings us into that fellowship. It is Jesus Christ and Him crucified that enables us to fellowship. That is the only way and the only possibility. Therefore, we need to know nothing save Jesus Christ and Him crucified. And if we do that, we will truly be one as He and the Father are one.

In the beginning of this letter to the Corinthians, we are amazed that Paul could say, "You all speak one word; be united in one mind and one opinion" (see 1:10). How can that be? If we are faithful to our calling and know nothing but Jesus Christ and Him crucified, then Christ is not divided. Otherwise, there will be division, not only in the world but in the church. And that is what we find in the first four chapters of the first letter to the Corinthians.

Incest in the Church

Now we would like to go into the second problem that the church in Corinth had. Again, it amazes us that this was not something the Corinthian believers inquired of Paul in their letter to him. Paul said, "This is something that is universally reported." In other words, when he talked about their division, he said the house of Chloe told him, but here he did not need anyone to tell him because it was something that was universally reported. It was known everywhere, so even when Paul was not in Corinth, he heard about it. It was well known. And strangely, the Corinthian believers did not even ask Paul about this problem because to them it was nothing. They were so dull in their conscience that they considered this thing as common, as nothing to worry about. But the apostle Paul, with his keen perception, his spirituality, his discernment, considered this as a most serious problem. It had to be addressed and dealt with.

The problem is incest. A brother in the church in Corinth took his father's wife, and this was something unknown even in the nations. And yet when this thing happened, the church at Corinth not only said nothing, they also did nothing! It was as if it was nothing to them. But when Paul heard of this, he saw that it was a serious breach to the fellowship of God's Son Jesus Christ. It was a contradiction and a serious violation to that sacred fellowship. It was so unholy, so unclean, and Paul's spirit was stirred. So he said, "Even though I am not with you in body I am with you in spirit, and I have judged this matter. And together with all of you I have committed this man to Satan that his body may be destroyed in order that his spirit might be saved."

The Feast of Unleavened Bread

Nevertheless, when Paul dealt with this situation, he took the higher ground. In other words, he was not just looking at this sin or other sins as you will find in chapter 6. He mentioned another sin among them. There was a brother who went to the court of the world to accuse another brother. But when Paul was dealing with all these negative things among God's people, he took the higher ground, that is to say, he looked at it from the standpoint of the positive of God's purpose, His heart and His will. Therefore, in this chapter he mentions this matter: "Let us celebrate the feast of unleavened bread." Now that is his approach.

We know that Paul said, "Our Passover, Christ Jesus has already been sacrificed." Thank God, when we have the Lord's Table, it is the reality of the Passover Feast that the children of Israel kept year after year—even today. When they were in Egypt as slaves, God redeemed them by the paschal lamb. Every family would prepare a spotless lamb, and on the 14th day of the month they would kill it and put the blood on the doorpost of their house. The entire family would gather within that house and eat the Passover lamb. While they were eating, at midnight the angel of destruction, who had come from God, passed through the whole land of Egypt to kill the firstborn of that land from Pharaoh to the slave, both man and animal, but when that angel saw blood on the door, he passed over. Therefore, it is called Passover, and because of the blood of the paschal lamb the children of Israel were spared.

Now we know this is a type and the antitype or the fulfillment is in our Lord Jesus Christ. God sent His only begotten Son into this world as the Lamb of God. He came to take away the sin of the world, and because of that He was slain on Calvary's cross, and His precious blood was shed. Our Passover Lamb has been sacrificed; therefore, the angel of destruction has passed over us. Our sins are forgiven and we are spared. We are redeemed by the blood of the Lamb. Satan and the world were judged, but we were delivered. That is Passover. And all of us have had our Passover.

The next day after Passover, the children of Israel had to keep the Feast of Unleavened Bread. As a matter of fact, these two feasts are together. In the New Testament, sometimes the Feast of Unleavened Bread is called the Passover Feast because they are one and the same thing. You cannot separate these two feasts. On the day of Passover you ate unleavened bread, and for seven days following that the children of Israel will eat only unleavened bread. In the house of the children of Israel there was to be no leaven whatsoever, so according to the custom of the Jews, before the Passover they had to search their house for any hidden leaven and purge it out. It was a most serious thing. In Exodus we are told that if anyone ate leaven during the Feast of Unleavened Bread he would be cut off from the commonwealth of Israel. In other words, he would be deprived of all the privileges of the covenant of God with the children of Israel. It was a serious thing.

Passover is just one day because our Lord Jesus was sacrificed once and for all. There cannot be a second Passover. It is only once and it is done forever. But the Feast of Unleavened Bread continues for seven days because seven in the Scripture represents perfection or fullness on this earth. In eternity the number is twelve but on earth it is seven. It is a perfect number, so it simply means that the Passover Feast was to be kept for one day but the Feast of the Unleavened Bread must be kept seven days. In other words, it is continuous. It is a life-time thing for us. With the children of Israel it was seven days but with the church it is a life-long feast. The church is celebrating the Feast of the Unleavened Bread, and we will celebrate that until the return of our Lord Jesus.

Purging out the Leaven

The apostle Paul says, "For also our passover, Christ, has been sacrificed" (I Corinthians 5:7b). We recognize that; we accept that; we believe that. But if we believe that, then what should we do following that Passover? "Let us celebrate the Feast of Unleavened Bread" (see v. 8). To put it simply, the church today is celebrating the Feast of Unleavened Bread. The church is a new lump or we can say it is a meal. It is three measures of meal to be offered to God as an oblation or food offering. We are in the days of celebrating the Feast of Unleavened Bread, so if there is any leaven in the church you can see how serious it is. It has to be purged because it is in contradiction to the meaning of Passover, which means our salvation. It is a contradiction to what God has done. And being the redeemed, we must keep the Feast of Unleavened Bread with sincerity and truth, not with malice and wickedness—not with leaven but with unleavened bread.

What is leaven? Leaven is not permitted to be offered to God with the meal offering. In other words, when you offer the meal offering—the flour, the bread, the loaf—you have to offer it to God without leaven. If it is with leaven it will not be accepted. In the offerings to God there are two things you cannot offer—leaven and honey. Leaven is something that you put into meal or flour, and it will begin to ferment. The flour will blow up or puff up, and the result is that the flour or the meal will become larger than it really is and softer, and is more tasty to people. That is why we use leaven when we make bread. I remember when I learned to make Chinese bread, I used leaven. I saw how the flour would puff up, and people liked to eat it. If it is unleavened, it is hard and difficult to digest, and it is not as tasty. That is the work of leaven with bread. But leaven in the Scripture always speaks of something evil or corrupt.

You remember in Matthew 16:6, 12, one day our Lord Jesus was with His disciples crossing the sea, and our Lord Jesus suddenly said, "Beware of the leaven of the Pharisees and the Sadducees.

The disciples said, "It is because we forgot to bring our bread." But our Lord Jesus said, "Don't you remember how many were fed by five loaves and two fish and how much bread was left? And you remember how on another occasion four thousand people were fed and how many baskets were left. I am not talking about this physical bread; I am talking about the doctrine of the Pharisees and the Sadducees."

The Doctrine of the Pharisees

What is the doctrine of the Pharisees? We know that the Pharisees are the strictest sect in Judaism. They make studying the Old Testament their life work. They not only study it, but they try to keep every letter of it. More than that, they believe and follow the teaching and the traditions of the fathers. In other words, when you open the Old Testament, you not only have the word of God but you have the principles. How are these principles to be applied? So throughout the years great rabbis were raised up, and they tried to interpret these Old Testament texts and made application of them. Suppose you said that on Saturday you should do no work. What is work? Well, if you are hungry and you go to a field of wheat you can pick the grain. That is not work, but you cannot rub it. If you rub it, that is work. On the Sabbath you can only walk a certain distance, and if you walk extra you are working. And in modern times, when you get into an elevator, if you push the button you are working. You cannot do that.

What is the doctrine or the leaven of the Pharisees? They blow up the word of God. They put something into it such as human thoughts, ideas, interpretations, and blow it up. They make it more than what it is, mixing truth with falsehood, human teaching with God's word until it suits the taste of people. When our Lord Jesus was on earth, He said, "You hypocrites, you keep the teaching of the traditions of the father and you violate the word of God." Who could dispute with these Pharisees, saying that they did not know the word? No, they knew the Scriptures. They were teachers, but they were not keeping the commandments. They mixed human tradition with God's pure word, and that is leaven.

The Leaven of the Sadducees

What is the leaven of the Sadducees? The Sadducees were another sect in Judaism. As a matter of fact, at the time of our Lord Jesus, the high priestly family were Sadducees. They were the rationalists. They rationalized the word of

God. If it did not appeal to their reasoning, they said it was not true. They did not believe in resurrection nor did they believe in spirit or angels. They did not believe it because it is beyond human reasoning. You could not say they did not believe in the Scriptures, because they studied the Old Testament and tried to keep the moral teaching and ethics in it. It is like people today who love the Sermon on the Mount, thinking that this is the highest ethical teaching in the world. But do they keep them? Or are they able to keep them? This is the leaven of the Sadducees. You cannot say they do not believe because they are a sect of Judaism. But if you say they believe, you discover that they do not really believe. Now that is where the confusion is.

Our Lord Jesus said, "Beware of the leaven of the Pharisees and the Sadducees." Why did He say this? If it is one hundred per cent error, everybody will know, and nobody will believe it. But if you mix error with truth, that is leaven. It blows up and puffs up, but it suits human taste. Therefore, the Lord Jesus makes it very clear that to celebrate the Feast of the Unleavened Bread is a life-long thing. So every sin, every wickedness, and every leaven has to be purged out.

Celebrate With the Bread of Sincerity and Truth

How do we keep the Feast of the Unleavened Bread? Remember that the Bible says, "Let us celebrate." It is a celebration. What do we celebrate? We celebrate something that the Lord Jesus has already accomplished for us. Think of that! He is our Passover Lamb. He has delivered us from sin, from the world, from our old man, from the flesh, from the old creation. He has delivered us completely. We are now a new lump, so we celebrate.

How do we celebrate the Feast of Unleavened Bread? It says, "Celebrate not with old leaven." We cannot celebrate with old leaven or with leaven of malice and wickedness, but with the unleavened bread of sincerity and truth. There is a contrast here. If we celebrate with malice and wickedness, that is the old leaven. If we celebrate with sincerity and truth, that is unleavened bread.

Malice and Truth

Malice and truth are opposite to each other. In the Chinese Bible malice is translated "hidden poison." It is a poison that is hidden. What is sincerity? Sincerity is transparency— completely open, nothing hidden and crystal clear.

What is wickedness? Wickedness is the opposite of truth. Whatever is not true in the sight of God is wickedness. Truth is the word of God; truth is Christ. Anything that is not Christ, anything that is not according to the word of God is untrue and is wickedness. So we cannot celebrate the Feast of the Unleavened Bread with malice and with wickedness. The only right way to celebrate is with sincerity and truth. There is nothing underground or hidden. It is pure, transparent, open, and according to the word of God.

The Work of the Cross

I want to ask one question. Why is it that the church in Corinth reacted in such a way with such a hideous sin in their midst? Why did they not mourn? Instead, they did nothing.

They considered it as very common; it is okay; it does not matter. Do we not know that if there is leaven, sooner or later the whole lump will be leavened? That is why you have to purge out the leaven. You cannot allow even a little leaven in because eventually it will pervade the whole lump. This is a most serious thing, and yet the Corinthian believers considered it as nothing. Why? The Corinthians were noted at that time for two things. One of them was their eloquence: "You speak like a Corinthian—eloquent." The other thing: "You live like a Corinthian—corrupt." That is what they were. But thank God, the blood of our Lord Jesus was shed. He washed their sins away, and they were sanctified and justified. Then why were they so negligent, that they could not consider this as something serious? On the contrary, probably they thought themselves as very liberal, open-hearted and loving. Basically it is because they did not take the cross of our Lord Jesus into their lives. They believed in the objective work of the cross, but they did not allow the cross to work in their own lives. They wanted to live an easy life, doing their own thing. Whatever they liked they wanted to do. They rejected the working of the cross in their life, and that is the reason the old leaven came out.

Right and Wrong Judging

Jesus Christ and Him crucified is so central to Christian life and to the church. If you do not talk about Jesus Christ and Him crucified, if you do not allow Jesus Christ and Him crucified to come into your life—not just a teaching— eventually it will be like the church in Corinth.

We are told in Matthew 7:1: "Judge not that ye might not be judged." If you judge others you will be judged, therefore do not judge. But if you read carefully the word of God there are two different kinds of judging. One kind is bad which is criticizing, despising, boasting, being arrogant, thinking that we are perfect and others are not. That kind of judging is forbidden because God is our judge. And if we judge people with that critical eye, the same judgment will eventually come upon us. But that does not mean we should not judge.

Matthew 7:1-2 says, "Judge not, that ye may not be judged; for with what judgment ye judge, ye shall be judged; and with what measure ye mete, it shall be measured to you." Then the Lord talked about a brother who had a mote in his eye, and someone goes to him and says, "I will cast the mote from your eye." I do thank the Lord that He was a carpenter, because in the carpenter's house, when they were doing woodwork, there were lots of these little things flying around that easily got into their eyes. So our Lord said, "If you go to your brother and tell him he has a mote in his eye and you want to take it out, remember you have a beam in your own eye. How dare you judge your brother! Judge yourself first. Take out the beam and then you can see clearer." Does that mean that we just let our brother go? No; then we help that brother take out the mote in his eye. It does not mean that we do nothing or say nothing, as if we have not seen. Not at all!

Judge also has another meaning. God wants us to judge which means to discern. We have to judge between good and evil, right and wrong. If there is no sense of such judgment, what kind of life is it? God is love, but He judges. We need to discern. Of course, we need to judge ourselves first, and if we allow the Holy Spirit to judge us and allow the cross to work in us, then we have the spiritual discernment to see what is going on in others, and we will have the ability to serve and minister to them. Without judgment there can be no ministry. Therefore, the Bible says the spiritual discerns all things. If we cannot discern, how can we help? How can we minister?

So there are two kinds of judgment. Notice the judgment of Paul when he said, "I am with you in spirit. My spirit and you are together. So judge in this matter and purge out that leaven." In other words, it is judging in the spirit and not in the flesh. If you judge in the flesh, that is wrong because you are arrogant. You think that you are perfect. Who are you to judge? But if it is in the spirit then there is humility, love, and ministry. That is the judgment we have to have. The church in Corinth had no judgment, and Paul had to touch their conscience to try to arouse them, in order that they may discern, judge, and even execute. Otherwise, if they allowed this thing to go on, sooner or later it would leaven the whole church. We must purge out the leaven.

When you read I Corinthians 5, you may think Paul was too harsh. "Deliver that person to Satan. Let his body be destroyed so that his spirit might be saved." There is love behind it.

Then in chapter 5:12 it says, "For what have I to do with judging those outside also? ye, do not ye judge them that are within?" In other words, we have no right to judge those who are without; God will judge them. But we have a moral responsibility to judge those who are within, those who are fellowshipping together. We need to judge one another; that is to say, we need to minister to one another and help one another towards celebrating with sincerity and truth. Otherwise we fail in our responsibility.

In chapter 6, Paul said, "Don't you know that one day we will judge the world?" The saints will judge the world. If today you are acting like the world, how can you judge the world in the day to come? If you are separated from the world, then you can judge the world. One day, God will give the judgment of the world to His Son and those who are with Him. Since we are chosen to judge the world, Paul could say, "Don't you have anyone among you that can judge among the brothers? Do the brothers have to go to the court of the world to get things settled? Are there no wise men among you? Why do you defraud your brother? Why are you not willing to be defrauded?" More than that, he said, "Don't you know we will even judge the angels?" Think of that! Angels are higher than man, and one day man will judge the angels. So what kind of purity and what kind of character must be built in man?

Truth and Love

Let us not be mistaken. There is nothing wrong in judging if it is in the right spirit. It is wrong if you do not judge. How can the parents raise up their children without judging? If there is no judging, there is no discipline. This is what you see today in this country. People believe that if you judge, you are not loving. And in order to love you need to not say anything, but just let people do whatever they want.

How twisted is our reasoning! In the word of God, you will find that truth and love are one. If there is truth, there is love. If there is love, there must be truth. You cannot love the untrue. If you love the untrue you really do not love; you hate.

Sometimes when you see a brother at fault, and then you remember your own experience of having been at fault but you repented and received the work of the cross in your life, if you say nothing or do nothing for your brother and just let it go, you hate your brother. You need to help your brother. The Bible says, "Those that are spiritual should help those who are weak, who may fall, but beware lest you also be tempted."

Our whole concept needs to be corrected. Today, we think that if we love then we do not care about the truth because if you tell the truth it will cause problems. People will react and be hurt. "Oh, don't hurt; it is all right; everything is okay; nothing is wrong." By talking in this way you actually "hate" your brother. What will happen when he shall appear before the judgment seat of Christ? We act like Cain: "Am I responsible for my brother?" God said, "You are responsible." Love sacrifices one's self in order to complete the others. That is love. That is the love of Christ; that is the love of God, and that is true love.

True Freedom

When I read I Corinthians 6:12, I wonder. I wonder if you wonder too. Why does Paul say, "All things are lawful to me, but all things do not profit; all things are lawful to me, but I will not be brought under the power of any." Why did Paul suddenly say these things? "All things are lawful to me." In other words, we were once under law, but thank God we are now under grace. And because we are under grace all things are lawful to us. Do we understand this? In other words, we are above the law, and because we are above the law, whatever we do is lawful. But even so he said, "But all things do not profit."

Yes, you are free. I remember in the early 60's during the days of "the sons of God" and all these things going on, people would go into a store and just take things without paying. Why? They would say, "We are sons of God; it all belongs to our Father. All things are lawful. We are free. We are above the law." Sometimes we interpret freedom in that way. All things are lawful to us; we are the redeemed of the Lord. We are sons of God and children of God, therefore we are above law, and we can do anything. All things are lawful, but remember, not all things are profitable. All things are lawful, but do not be brought under the power of any. If you are brought under the power of any, you become slaves. You are no longer the sons of God; you have become slaves.

How often we interpret our liberty in such a way. This is abusing the liberty that God has given to us. Maybe the Corinthian believers say, "Thank God, we are saved; we are above the law, so all things are lawful. We can do anything." And Paul said, "Now remember, the law is profitable. If it is not profitable, do not do it. If you are brought under its power, do not do it."

What is true liberty or true freedom? We are free from sin, we are free from the world, and we are even free from ourselves—our flesh. We are free to worship God, and we are free to serve Him. That is true freedom.

The Corinthian church had leaven among them, yet they were not conscious of it. Their conscience had to be aroused in order for them to purge out that leaven and keep the feast with sincerity and truth.

In II Corinthians many commentators believe that the man Paul mentioned had been judged by all the brothers and sisters, that he had been convicted and he had repented. Then Paul said, "Forgive him; receive him." Most likely, that man he referred to was the same man who had committed this incest. So may the Lord have mercy upon His church. May He preserve His church from corruption, and may He have a glorious church, holy, blameless, without spot or wrinkles of any sort. God have mercy upon us.

6—Do All Things to God's Glory

I Corinthians 10:31-33—Whether therefore ye eat, or drink, or whatever ye do, do all things to God's glory. Give no occasion to stumbling, whether to Jews, or Greeks, or the assembly of God. Even as I also please all in all things; not seeking my own profit, but that of the many, that they may be saved.

When you read I Corinthians, you may think that it is a very negative letter because it deals with a great deal of negative things. But I believe that I Corinthians is very positive because at the very outset he sets before us that we are called into the fellowship of God's Son Jesus Christ. And there is nothing more glorious than this calling. Think of that. Sometimes we look upon the Corinthian believers and wonder how they can be believers in such an unbelieving state. But we have to think of ourselves because even so, we are all called into that wonderful, glorious, heavenly fellowship—the fellowship that the Son has with His Father and the Father with His Son. And now this fellowship has been extended even to us, the redeemed of the Lord, in order that we may share in common with God, with Christ, and with one another. And I think there is nothing higher than that. It is not a theory or a doctrine or a teaching; it is a fellowship. And fellowship is living and real, and we are all called into that fellowship.

The reason the Corinthians had so many problems is because they were not living in that fellowship of God's Son.

These are problems that are against that fellowship, and if they had only lived in that fellowship all these problems would have been solved. And the apostle Paul is trying to tell them how these problems can be solved in a positive way.

In the six chapters we have covered they had two very serious problems. But strangely, the Corinthian believers did not even ask Paul about these problems. In other words, they did not think these were problems, but actually, they were the biggest problems. One of the problems Paul had heard from the house of Chloe, and the other problem was universally reported.

The first problem was division. Think of that! Division cuts across the very meaning of fellowship. Fellowship brings us together into one. It is sharing the same life with one another. Division breaks up that fellowship. The reason for breaking up is because they did not center upon Christ Jesus and Him crucified. Our fellowship is around Jesus Christ and nobody else. We are not fellowshipping around Paul, or Peter, or Apollos, or anybody else. We are fellowshipping in Christ Jesus, with Christ Jesus, and with all who are in Christ Jesus. That is what we share in common. And if we want to share Christ Jesus, we have to know Him crucified, because it is through the cross that Christ is given to us. And it is only by the working of the cross in our lives that we are able to truly fellowship in Christ Jesus and not in ourselves nor in others. So the biggest problem is division, and the way to solve it is to see Jesus Christ and Him crucified.

The second problem was universally reported, and yet the Corinthian believers were not even conscious of it as a problem. They allowed such things to go on without any correction, without any discipline, as if it was nothing. And it was something that even the world had rarely seen; it was incest. So the apostle Paul dealt with this problem, and again he dealt with it in a positive way. He said, "Christ our Passover has been slain, and we are now in the Feast of Unleavened Bread." How can we celebrate the Feast with the leaven of corruption, whether it is moral corruption or teaching corruption? We have to be a pure meal offered to God. That is what the fellowship is; that is what the church is. And if we celebrate it in the right way, such moral corruption will be dealt with.

Problems in the Corinthian Church

Now we would like to cover four chapters, from chapters 7- 10. I have put this matter of sexual life and social life together, and that is why we have the four chapters. Beginning from chapter 7, Paul began to answer the questions that the Corinthian believers asked of him. Finally, we see some of the problems that they had among themselves. In chapter 7:1 he said, "But concerning the things of which ye have written to me."

In chapter 7 there is this matter of marriage and their sex life. In chapter 8 they asked about things sacrificed to idols. They asked about eating and drinking, and social life. This continues on to chapter 10. Then in chapter 12 they asked about this matter of the spirituals, which is what it says in the original, and it deals with gifts. In chapter 16 they asked about collections.

Before the Corinthian believers believed in the Lord Jesus, they were noted for two things. They were noted for their intelligence because they were very intelligent and knowledgeable. They were also eloquent. Now some people may have knowledge but not eloquence. But the Corinthians had both knowledge and eloquence. They were also noted for their moral corruption. So people had sayings in those days: "You speak like the Corinthians." In other words, they were very eloquent and very intelligent. "Also," they said, you live like the Corinthians because you have a very corrupt and immoral life." That is what the Corinthians used to be. But thank God, they had been justified, sanctified, and they had been redeemed of the Lord. After they were saved and came into the fellowship of God's Son Jesus Christ, naturally some problems occurred, and these are what they asked about.

Sexual Life and Social Life

They asked first of all about their sexual life. After they were saved, how should they live their sexual life? And they also asked about social life. After they were saved, how should they eat? How should they drink? How should they continue with their social relationships? These were very practical questions. We who are saved by the Lord, we who have lived for many years in the past and now we are saved, how should we live our sexual life? How should we live our social life? I wonder if we have ever asked such a question. We should.

And then you find another thing. I do not know if I am just reading something into it or whether there was something in it, but why did the Corinthian believers ask these questions? They had allowed incest and moral corruption to continue among them, and they never asked any questions. Why did they ask about it now? They had enjoyed their social life all along, so why should they ask questions about eating and drinking? Evidently, there was something challenging the way that they lived within them. They asked these questions because they still wanted to continue on with their old way of living. Now I wonder if I am reading something into it or not.

When God created us, it was not as one individual. He said, "It is not good for man to be alone." Man is made up of male and female. In other words, God created us as social beings. We are not supposed to live all by ourselves. We are to live with other people, either in the family or in society. Human beings are gregarious; we belong to one another. We are not just one single individual. That is the way God created us. God created us as male and female. There is nothing wrong with that because it is from God.

God created us with the desire to eat and drink, otherwise we cannot live. That is the way we have been created, and that is the way we have been living all along. When we come into the fellowship of God's Son Jesus Christ, how does it affect us? Are we going to be monks and nuns? Are we going to be hermits? Is that the way to live the Christian life? The very word *fellowship* tells us we are to be together and sharing together.

Spiritual-Human

Sometimes we have a wrong feeling about what it means to be spiritual. Our sensing can be in two extremes. One extreme is to think that the way we lived before we were saved is the same way we should live after we are saved. Before we were saved, we lived in such a way, and after we are saved, we still live in that same way. That is one extreme.

The other extreme is to think that after we are redeemed and belong to the fellowship of God's Son Jesus Christ, we are now supposed to be spiritual, which means to be less human or inhuman.

I remember our dear brother Watchman Nee said to us, "If you do not know how to be human, how can you be spiritual?" There is no conflict between being human and spiritual. As a matter of fact, unless you are human you cannot be spiritual. But human does not mean fallen human; it means redeemed human. God created us with a purpose, and to be a real human is to be living as the man and woman that God has created and that means being spiritual. That is the God's purpose in creating us. Therefore, do not think that now we are saved and belong to the fellowship of God's Son Jesus Christ, we have to be inhuman because this will make us more spiritual than we are. It is exactly the opposite. Is it because of that we can live our old way of life, continue with moral corruption, satisfying our lusts and passions without any control, without any discipline, and live a dissipated and immoral life? Should we continue to live our old way even in our family, in our home, or even in society? What should we do? Should there be any change? And in what way should there be change? These are very practical questions. And here, the apostle Paul is trying to answer them and lead them in a positive way.

After we are saved, it does not mean we are no longer human beings. We are on our way to being real human and real spiritual. You cannot divide these two things. On the other hand, we should be clear that now we have a new life—the life of Christ, a holy life, sanctified, separated, heavenly, spiritual—in our sexual and social life, there must be a change.

Christ Life vs. Adamic Life

Unfortunately, God's people tend to compartmentalize their life. Our lives do touch and cover many areas. We have our personal life when we are by ourselves. We have our family life when we are in the family with a husband and wife, father and mother, children, brothers and sisters. We have our social life, and we work in the world in contact with people (as a matter of fact, fellowship is social, but it is on a higher level). We still continue to live in all these areas, but how sad that many of God's people try to compartmentalize their lives. They live a personal life different from their family life. Their family life is different from their social life. And their social life is different from their church life. They put them into different compartments and live them with different lives.

Now we have at least two lives; we have the life of Christ in us, and we have the life that we inherited from Adam. And sometimes we use our Adamic life to apply in all these so-called unspiritual areas and only apply spiritual life, Christ life, to church life. When we go to church we become spiritual; we begin to live by that life that is holy, spiritual, heavenly, uncommon, unique, and different. But when we are home or work or society, we are a different person. This is not what the Lord wants us to be. There is only one life. Formerly we lived by that old Adamic life, and that life lived alone, lived with the parents, lived with the children, lived with husband and wife, and lived in society. Now we have a different life, eternal life, the life of Christ. And can it be that we only live the life of Christ in the church and still live our old life alone or in the family or in society? If so we are hypocrites. May the Lord deliver us from being hypocrites. There is only one life that we live—whether we are alone, in the family, in society, or in the church. Are we living by that one life?

Positive Principles

The Corinthians thought that they could compartmentalize their lives. In the church, you behave one way, but in the family, all by yourself, or in society, you can still live your old life. This is the wrong way. So here the apostle Paul lays down certain positive principles: "Do all things to God's glory." All things include eating, drinking, sexual life, family life, social life, everything. "Do all things to God's glory."

"Give no occasion to stumbling." Do not stumble anybody, whether they are Jews, Greeks, or the church of God.

"Not seeking my own profit, but that of the many, that they may be saved." Always seek the eternal salvation of others.

Free To Choose

In our marriage or family life, we need to live by the life of Christ in us. So in chapter 7 we see that Paul is trying to tell us something. Do not think that because you believe in the Lord Jesus, you are in bondage. I am afraid that many believers have that kind of false thinking: "Formerly we were free to do anything we wanted to do. Now that we believe in the Lord Jesus, we are under bondage. We cannot do this; we should not do that." Actually it is just the opposite. Before we believed in the Lord Jesus, we were in bondage. We were not free. We were slaves to sin, we were slaves to the world, and followed the current of the world. We drifted along with the current because we could not resist it. There was no power in us. We were under the power of darkness, and we were not free. We were slaves just like the Israelites in Egypt who had no freedom. But thank God, we are now free. He has freed us. We are not under law but under grace, and this simply means that we are now free to choose. Formerly, we could not choose because we were under law and in bondage. But now we can choose. Formerly, we could not choose not to sin, but now we can choose not to sin. Formerly, we could not choose to do the right thing, but now we can. Our Lord Jesus has set us free.

"All things are lawful but all things are not profitable. All things are lawful, but I will not come under the bondage of anything." Think of that! We are now living on a higher ground, under a higher law, and we are no longer under bondage. We are a free people. We can sin if we want to. We can live our old life if we want to. We can still live our old way of social life if we want to. We can do that, but on the other hand, we can do otherwise. We can live as God wants us to live. We can live for the glory of God so that in everything we glorify the Lord. Even in our personal life, in our home, in society, in the church, we may do all things to the glory of God. People think to be free is to do anything you like, but real freedom is that you are free to do what God wants you to do.

The Royal Law of Love

The apostle Paul shows us that in Christ there is liberty. It is a law of liberty, and it is the royal law of love. And if you love you fulfill all the law. So do remember that we are free, and because we are free we choose the higher ground. We choose to do all things to the glory of God.

The Corinthian believers liked to be social, and in those days, most social activities were carried on in the idol temples. The best and the cheapest meat was the meat that had been sacrificed to the idols. The priests would sell it in the market for the cheapest price, and if you wanted to eat the best meat, it was that meat that had been sacrificed to idols. If you wanted to eat and drink and enjoy a social gathering, you would go to the temple; otherwise you would be isolated.

So the Corinthian believers liked social life which included parties, and all of them were carried on in the temple. They enjoyed the best of food and drink that was available. Then they got saved. Now what should they do? Should they go to the temple to eat? Should they still join with the others and eat meat sacrificed to idols? The Corinthian believers were very knowledgeable, and they said, "We know there is only one God. All these so-called gods are nothing; therefore things sacrificed to nothing are nothing. So we can eat this meat that has a cheap price. Since the temple offers to the idols, the idols are nothing. The temple is just another building; that is all. So we can go to the temple and enjoy ourselves."

Is that good, solid, sound knowledge? Yes, we have only one God. We have only one Lord, our Lord Jesus Christ, and all the other things are just nothing. That is very correct. But Paul said, "You want to enjoy yourself, and you can, but you forget that you are not alone. There are other brothers and sisters who have weak consciences. They worshiped the idols before and made offerings to them, eating what was offered to the idols. Now they are saved, and they feel that all these are unclean. They do not want to go to the temple, and they do not want to touch these things sacrificed to idols. But when they see you going into the temple and enjoying yourself by eating and drinking, they say, "Well, if you can do that, I can do it too." So they did it with an evil conscience. Their conscience had been bribed but it was evil. It bothered them, and yet they did it.

You have stumbled your brothers. In other words, we who are the Lord's do not live for ourselves—we live for others. We do not live by our knowledge—we live by love. Knowledge puffs up, but love edifies and builds up. True, you have the knowledge but you are puffed up: "Why can't I do it? I know it and I enjoy it." But you forget that you are stumbling your brother who has a weak conscience, and sinning against your brother is sinning against the Lord. We do not live by knowledge but by love. And love thinks not of itself. It thinks of others—what is best for our brothers and sisters.

Even in our social life, do we just live for ourselves? Why do we want a social life? Why do we want parties? Why do we want eating and drinking? We want to enjoy ourselves. But do we ever think of our weaker brothers and sisters? Maybe what we are doing stumbles our weaker brothers and sisters, and if that is the case we sin against the Lord.

So the apostle Paul said, "Even if your knowledge is correct, you do not live by your knowledge; you live by love." As a matter of fact, even what you consider as correct knowledge is incorrect because you cannot drink the cup of the Lord and the cup of the demons; you cannot eat the bread of the Lord and the bread of the demons. So it is still incorrect. No matter how logical you think it is, it is still illogical in the sight of God.

We are living on a higher ground, and we are under a higher law. We are free to do anything, but we are able to choose the right thing. So the apostle Paul illustrated this to us. He said, "If I eat meat and my brother will be stumbled, I will not eat meat anymore." We should eat meat. God does not want us to be vegetarians, but the apostle Paul is willing to let go of his rights. He has many rights. He said, "I can take a wife to travel with me like the other apostles. I can live by preaching the gospel like the others, but I do not do it. I am willing not to seek my right if only I can save some." He lived for the others, for their eternal good. And this is love.

Running the Race

So in these chapters the apostle Paul tries to tell us that life is a race, and we are running in that race. When we are saved, God puts us on the race course of faith, and now we are running that race. And when we run a race, we need to have a mindset to run to win. That is the way to run. Otherwise, halfway, maybe a third, or just a few steps, and we will drop out. When we run, we have a goal before us, and we set our heart upon it. Paul said, "Thus run." That is the way to run. We do not run without a goal and just drift along.

Do we have a goal before us? The apostle Paul in Philippians tells us that he forgets what lies behind and presses on toward the goal to win the prize, and the prize is Christ. It is to win Christ. Thus run.

Life consists of wrestling. Therefore, when we wrestle, we have to obey certain rules. This means discipline—living a disciplined life. Paul said, "I put my body under." In the original it says, "I beat it black and blue and do not allow my body to rule over me. I do not live for my body; I live for Christ, lest I preach to others and I myself am cast away" (see I Corinthians 9:24-27).

This is the mindset we should have. C. T. Studd said, "Christians, today, are chocolate soldiers." We are drifting. There is no more time. Be vigilant, be diligent, watch, and pray, for the days are closing.

Paul tried to help us that we may really be in the fellowship of God's Son Jesus Christ, and it touches every area of our life. May the Lord help us.

7—The Breaking of Bread

I Corinthians 14:40—But let all things be done comelily and with order [Or, in some versions it says, "properly, fittingly, decently, harmoniously, and with an orderly manner."]

We have been considering together on this first letter to the Corinthians. Basically, this letter is focused on one thing: we are called into the fellowship of God's Son Jesus Christ. That is where we are today. We all have been called by the grace of God through the finished work of Christ into the fellowship that our Lord Jesus has with His Father. Now it has been extended to us so that we may be in the good of that fellowship, sharing with God, sharing with Christ, and sharing with one another. And what a privilege that is! The church in Corinth was full of problems, and, basically, all these problems were due to the fact that they did not truly know the fellowship of God's Son Jesus Christ. To put it another way, all these are problems concerning the fellowship of God's Son Jesus Christ. In the past, we have mentioned a number of them—this matter of division, moral corruption, and social matters that were not according to God. In other words, even though the Bible says these Corinthian believers were saved, they were sanctified, they were justified, yet they did not live up to that fellowship. Oftentimes, they fell back into their old ways and lived by their old natural life. As a result of that, all these problems came into their midst.

Church Life

We would like to continue on with I Corinthians 11 through chapter 16 because, in these chapters, we find one common subject—church life, assembly life, body life. We are called into the fellowship of God's Son Jesus Christ. What is it? You remember when our Lord Jesus was on earth, in view of Calvary He told His disciples: "On this rock, I will build My church, and the gates of Hades shall not prevail against it." We know that the very word *church* in the Greek original is *ekklesia* and it means "called out ones gathered together." So we can say that church life is a gathering together life. In Hebrews 10:25, we are exhorted not to forsake the assembling of the saints, especially in view of the day drawing nigh. So in our calling this church life, assembling life, body life occupies a very important part. We mentioned before that life is multidimensional. In other words, we live our lives in many different areas which include the personal life, the family life, and the social life. And we as believers have a church life, an assembling life, a body of Christ life to live. As a matter of fact, this area is the most important because when you look at the eternal purpose of God, we see that He is after a corporate body. He is after a bride or we may say a collective entity. So after the Corinthian believers believed in the Lord Jesus, they did gather together. But when they gathered together, they found many problems. As a matter of fact, in the last six chapters of this letter, they asked the apostle Paul some questions. For instance, in chapter 12:1, they asked Paul about this matter of spirituals. They wanted to know how to be really spiritual and how to exercise their spiritual gifts. Then in chapter 16, they asked Paul about this matter of collection and about giving. Now these are questions that relate to church life, assembly life, and body life. So Paul realized the importance of church life; therefore he enlarged it. Instead of just answering their two questions he began to include in his reply questions they had not asked. Paul realized that these were very, very important questions and things that needed to be adjusted. Therefore, the last six chapters of I Corinthians are devoted to this area of church life, assembly life, and body life.

The Ruling Principle Of Church Life

Can we see some ruling or governing principle concerning this matter of church life? I think the Scripture we read probably is that governing principle: "Let all things be done comelily and with order." In other words, church life is the expression of the life of Christ. Now we can express the life of Christ personally, we should express the life of Christ in our family life, and we should let the life of Christ regulate our social life. However, in church life it is the corporate expression of the life of Christ. Or we could say: it is the life of Christ expressed and manifested among those who are His. Therefore, if church life is the life of Christ in a corporate expression, what is the ruling principle behind Christ's life? In John 1:14 it says, "The Word became flesh and tabernacled among men, full of grace and truth." In other words, His life is full of grace and truth. His life is so gracious, so beautiful, so harmonious, so wonderful, so truthful and orderly. There is no confusion, and there is no mixture. It is pure, clean, heavenly, and spiritual. Now that is the life of Christ that we see lived out in His person, and this same life that is in us together must be lived in the same way. So the ruling principle of church life is comelily and orderly, and it is full of grace and truth. It is an expression of Christ himself. God is not a God of disorder but of order. Our God is a God of beauty. Everything is so harmonious—there is nothing mixed or confused. And that is the way church life is to be. Paul realized the importance of church life and he used six chapters to give instructions to the Corinthian believers. Beginning with chapter 11, the first thing he addresses is head covering. He wants us to see that there is a divine order. God is the head of Christ; Christ is the head of every man; and man is the head of the woman. Then there is the matter of the breaking of bread. After that he addresses the subject of spiritual gifts and how to exercise spiritual gifts in the meeting. Then he takes up the matter of collection or giving. How should believers give? Then there is the matter of obedience and submission. All these problems are related to church life. We would like to share together on this matter of the breaking of bread. The breaking of bread is a most important expression of corporate life. In the book of Acts the Holy Spirit described the church life that these people began to live. At first there were one hundred and twenty believers, and then on the day of Pentecost three thousand joined them. Later on it increased and increased and increased. How did they live together? What kind of church life did they have? How did they assemble? How did the body of Christ exercise itself?

Teaching of the Apostles

You will find it in a simple sentence in Acts 2:42: "They all continued in the teaching and the fellowship of the apostles in breaking of bread and prayers." That can include every thing in fellowship life. They continued, persevered in the teaching and the fellowship of the apostles. Now we all know that the apostles do not have their own teachings. The teachings of the apostles are one—it is the teaching of Christ. They never taught anything that they had not received from the Lord. It is what they saw, what they heard, and what they learned from the Lord that they passed on to us. Paul does not have his own teaching; Peter does not have his own teaching; James does not have his own teaching. It is true that their teaching seems to have different emphasis and touches different areas. But whatever they taught is what they had received from the Lord. It is the teaching of the Lord Jesus.

Fellowship of the Apostles

"And fellowship of the apostles …" The apostles did not have their own fellowships. When the Corinthian believers tried to create a Pauline fellowship, Paul said, "Who am I? Did I die for you? Are you baptized in my name?" There was no such thing as a Pauline fellowship, or a Petrine fellowship, or an Apollos fellowship. No such thing! Even though there were many apostles, in I John 1 the apostle John said, "Our fellowship is with the Father and with the Son, and now we pass on our fellowship. We report it to you that you too may have fellowship with us." In other words, there is only one fellowship, and it is fellowshipping on the Lord Jesus Christ.

The Expression of Church Life

How did they express and how did they continue in the teaching and the fellowship of the apostles? It was especially in two things—the breaking of bread and prayer. This shows us how important the breaking of bread and prayer are in the church. It is not private prayer or personal prayer, but it is corporate prayer. The church comes together to break bread, and the church comes together to pray. You cannot break the bread alone. You need at least a plurality of two because it is a corporate thing. So in the early church they really emphasized this matter of breaking of bread. As a matter of fact, you find in Acts 2 that they broke bread every day, at every meal, and from house to house because this is the noblest, fullest expression of church life. Throughout church history this has continued on, even though we find later on it became a tradition. It has lost its real meaning. Nevertheless, it is something that has continued even unto this day because on the night of His betrayal, before His crucifixion, our Lord Jesus gathered His own disciples in that upper room. They ate the Passover Feast, and during that supper the Lord Jesus took the bread, blessed it, broke it, and gave it to His disciples. He said, "This loaf is My body; do this in remembrance of Me." Then after the supper, He took the cup, blessed it, and He gave it to His disciples and said, "This is the cup of the new covenant in My blood; do this in remembrance of Me." Since that night, instead of celebrating Passover, the church has been celebrating the breaking of bread. It is not a ritual nor is it a tradition; it is something real, living, spiritual, and heavenly. The Corinthian believers did gather together to break bread, but hear what Paul said: "In this matter I do not praise you because when you gather together, it is not for better but for worse." Can you gather together for worse instead of for better? Paul said, "I understand that there are divisions and sects in your midst. A sect simply means "different schools of opinions." In other words, this breaking of bread is a symbol of oneness, but you have come together with divisions, with different opinions, and with different hearts. You are not one, so when you gather together it is not for better but for worse. In the early days the church combined the meal and breaking of bread together because it happened at the last supper. In Acts 2 they broke bread at every meal, and then later on in Acts it was once on the Lord's day. But at first, the Corinthian believers put these two things together. And because of their divisions, their different opinions, and not being one in the spirit, this was even expressed in their eating. People who were rich would have a rich meal before the brothers and sisters, and people who were poor had nothing to eat and were starving. Some were drinking and even drunk, but others were starving. And Paul said, "You gather for worse, not for better." But we know that later on they separated the love feast and breaking of bread and they became two different things instead of doing them together. The Corinthian believers kept the tradition, but they kept it in the wrong way. And it is serious because Paul said, "There are many who are weak and even some who die." Somehow the judgment of God was upon them. So the important thing is we need to know what the breaking of bread really is so that we will not take it lightly and drink and eat our own sin. On the other hand, we need to know what to do when we come together to break bread. As you read I Corinthians 11:17-33, you will find that Paul actually was trying to tell them that they had made the breaking of bread so elaborate that it was more than what it really is. In other words, we human beings tend to make simple things complicated. God's truth is very simple. There is the simplicity which is of Christ, and the enemy tries to entice us away from it. Therefore, if you look at the so-called breaking of bread today, whatever name it might be called—a mass as the Catholics call it, sacrament, or holy communion—it has become a very elaborate thing. There are lots of rituals and lots of rules instead of it being an expression of the life of Christ— free but orderly and beautiful.

What is the Breaking of Bread?

Remembrance

Paul is trying to tell them what the reality of breaking of bread is. It is very simple. All we are commanded to do is just this—the loaf and the cup. And we need to know what the loaf represents and what the cup represents. We need to know what we are doing. On the night of His betrayal, the Lord Jesus took that loaf, blessed it, broke it, delivered it to us and said, "This is My body broken for you. Do this in remembrance of Me." Throughout church history there have been so many theories about this loaf. Some take it as the literal body of Christ. After the priests bless it, this loaf, which is made of meal, becomes the literal body of Christ, and they sacrifice the body of Christ once more. They crucify Him again and again and again. Other people take it as a symbol. It is a loaf, and nothing but a loaf. It only represents the body of Christ; it is not the real body of Christ. So when you take a piece, you do not need to be too serious about it because it is just a loaf. What is it? The Lord said, "This is My body." Do you take it literally? Or do you take it symbolically? How do you take it? Remember, this breaking of bread is a spiritual thing, and therefore we cannot look at it either literally or symbolically. We have to look at it spiritually. In other words, the loaf is still a loaf but in our spirit we remember Him and His body broken for us. So we have to take it spiritually. And when we look at this loaf, we remember the holy body of the Lord Jesus. He lived thirty-three and a half years in such holiness, sanctified, set apart totally for God. There was never a sin; He does not even know what sin is. He pleased His Father in that body, and that pure body was broken for us. What love is behind it! Can you take this loaf and not be melted by His love? Take it spiritually. It means a great deal, much more than we think. More than that, we remember what we have seen and heard and experienced in the past. We cannot remember something that we have not experienced. That is the reason only those who are truly redeemed of the Lord can partake in this loaf and in this cup because it is a remembrance. If you do not remember and have no experience of how Christ died for you when you were in your sins, and if you do not remember that you are saved, redeemed, and know Him as your Savior and Lord, then there is no way you can remember the Lord. You have nothing to remember. So to remember, you need to really know Him and that His body was broken for you.

Exhibit the Death of Christ

Not only that, in I Corinthians 11:26, it tells us: "For as often as ye shall eat this bread, and drink the cup, ye announce the death of the Lord." Remembering is looking back. We have something to remember. We look back to the time when the Lord opened our eyes and saw how the sinless One died for our sins. We remember. But we not only remember when we come together to break the bread and drink the cup, we also announce the death of Christ. We exhibit the death of the Lord. When we look at the table and see the bread on one side and the cup on the other side, it means that when the blood is separated from the body, that is death. So you exhibit before the world, even before the unseen world, the death of the Lord. That is our testimony. We are here today because of the death of the Lord. We proclaim what the death of the Lord has done, and this is our testimony to the world and even to the unseen world, to the angels, and even to the demons. It is a testimony in this present time. Every time we come to remember the Lord, we announce, "This is our testimony." We are what we are today. We gather together today because of what the death of the Lord has done for us. We are not ashamed to declare it and let the whole world know that our Lord Jesus has died for us.

Looking to His Coming

Furthermore, He said, "Until I come." That is looking to the future. We are here breaking this bread, drinking this cup to remember what the Lord has done for us, to exhibit and to announce His finished work to the whole world. And we are here to break the bread until the day when He shall come again. Our Lord Jesus told His disciples on that night, "For I say unto you, that I will not drink at all of the fruit of the vine until the kingdom of God come" (Luke 22:18). So there is something we are looking forward to. We are looking forward to His return. He has risen; He has ascended. He is now at the right hand of His Father, and He is coming back to receive us. We will have this Lord's supper until He comes, and then we will have the marriage feast of the Lamb. Think of that! This is what the Lord's supper really means.

The Lord's Table

More than that, in I Corinthians 10:16-22 we find something different. In chapter 11 the breaking of bread is called the Lord's supper because supper is the time when the whole family gathered together. But in chapter 10 it is called the Lord's table. In the Bible table represents fellowship, sharing together. Therefore, it calls it, "The Lord's table." And even the order is different. In chapter 11 we see that the Lord Jesus is the One who blessed the loaf and the cup. But in chapter 10 we bless the cup and the loaf. In chapter 11 the bread comes first, and the cup comes next. In chapter 10 the cup comes first and the bread comes next. Do you see the distinction there? It speaks of the same thing, but it gives a different angle. In chapter 11 it is the Lord who gives this to us, and in chapter 10 it is we who respond to Him. So far as our experience goes, the blood is before the bread. So far as God's purpose is concerned, the bread comes before the blood, because if there is no body, where is the blood? But our experience is first His blood, the redeeming, the atoning, and then we experience His life. So that is why in chapter 10 it is called the Lord's table.

Communion in the Blood

"The cup of blessing which we bless ..." It is the communion of the blood of Christ. Communion is the same word as fellowship but when we talk about communion with God or fellowship with God, in our mind it does not seem too pious. Actually it is the same word. So here the emphasis is on communion, sharing together, experiencing. Every time you drink the cup you share the same with Christ. You experience once more the wonderfulness of the cleansing and the forgiving of your sins. It refreshes you, reinvigorates you, and enables you to continue on your pilgrimage. Every time you come to the Lord's table, it strengthens you because it is real and living.

Communion of the Body of Christ

"And the communion of the body of Christ …" When you take that loaf, you experience once more the abundant supply of His life. From now on you can live by His life. You have the strength to continue on your pilgrimage. There is a spiritual experience going on. It is not a ritual nor is it something you can take lightly. There is something real, spiritual and living going on. Do you really receive the benefit of it? If only we could break the bread as God has ordained it, what a difference it will make to us.

Come in a Worthy Manner

Because of this we are exhorted not to come in an unworthy manner. We say the Lord is worthy. What does it mean? If you say the Lord is worthy, do you come to Him in a worthy manner, worthy of His worthiness? If the President of the United States invited you to dinner, how would you go? Would you prepare yourself for that occasion? Would you take a bath? Would you put on your best clothes and act in your best manner? Of course, you would because he is the President. He is a worthy man, and you can only go to him in a worthy manner. You cannot go there barefoot and naked. That is what the Corinthians did. They went to the Lord's supper in a totally unworthy manner of the Lord. Are we any better? This is very real. It breaks the heart of our Lord when we think of the way we come to the Lord's supper. In some places, when they have communion, they have a special time for people to come together and get ready for it. Now I do not advocate that because we should be ready every moment. But do we come prepared? If the President of the United States invited you for dinner at eight o'clock, would you show up at nine o'clock? Is that a worthy manner? In one sense, we are never worthy. We are like Mephibosheth, who was the enemy of David. In the love of God and because of his covenant with Jonathan, David received Mephibosheth, his enemy, as his own son. And when Mephibosheth was at the table of David, those crippled legs were under the table. That is what we are. When we come to the Lord's table, thank God we are treated as sons and daughters. We are having a love feast with our Lord Jesus himself. He invites us to drink of Him and eat of Him, but our crippled legs are always under the table because we are sinners saved by grace. We are never worthy, but thank God He makes us worthy. It is all grace, but can we abuse that grace because of this? We still need to come in a worthy manner. What is a worthy manner? In I Corinthians 11:28-29 it says, "So that whosoever shall eat the bread, or drink the cup of the Lord, unworthily, shall be guilty in respect of the body and of the blood of the Lord. But let a man prove himself, and thus eat of the bread, and drink of the cup. For the eater and drinker eats and drinks judgment to himself, not distinguishing the body."

Distinguish the Body

First of all, to come in a worthy manner is distinguishing the body. In other words, you know what you are doing. You know what this body represents. You are not just coming to an ordinary meal; you are coming to the Lord's table. You are coming to the Lord's supper. He invites you to come, and the first thing you need to do is distinguish the body. What does it mean? We have already said that this loaf represents the body in two ways. Before it is broken it represents the personal body of Christ which is the body He took upon himself in His incarnation: "The Word became flesh." In that body He lived thirty-three and a half years, and He gave up that body for us. So whenever you come to the Lord's table, distinguish the body. This is the body of Christ. It is not something common. Spiritually you have to distinguish the body, and that will give you a kind of seriousness. You cannot come lightly when you think it represents the body of Christ. After the bread is broken, you take a piece and I take a piece. When we look on the table, that loaf is gone; it has disappeared. But it has not disappeared because it reappears among all those who have taken a piece. In other words, that body represents the church. So in I Corinthians 10 it says, "We being many are one loaf or one body." When God looks down from heaven He sees that one loaf in us. We are many but we are one. That is the body. That is the reason when we break the bread we need to remember this. This loaf not only represents the body of Christ personally but also corporately. It does not just represent the few of us here. Whenever we break the bread, we are not only in fellowship with Christ because it is His body—but we are also in fellowship with all of the believers in the world. They may not be here but our fellowship includes them. This bread is never exclusive but it is all inclusive. As we distinguish the body, it broadens our heart.

Prove Yourself

"Let a man prove himself." What does it mean? It means examine yourself or scrutinize yourself. Put yourself in the light of God's word so that when you come to take the loaf and the cup, if there is any controversy between you and the Lord that has not been settled, you know it. Is there any hatred, any enmity between you and any brother or sister before you come to the Lord's table? All these need to be settled before you take the loaf and the cup. Prove yourself. That is why we need to come prepared and not just casually. I remember a true story. One man killed another man's father, and that man determined he would avenge his father. After some years, this man got saved. He traveled to a place where there was a gathering of the saints, and it was the Lord's day and they were having the Lord's table. When he went in and sat down, he saw his enemy whom he had determined to kill. He struggled. He had met his enemy, and he wanted to kill him. He got up and walked out because he did not know what to do. This man was now a brother in the Lord, but he still wanted to kill him. That was his vow, and he did not know what to do. He did not feel that he could break bread with him, so he walked out. He prayed and asked the Lord what he should do. He knew that he could not go back with an unforgiving spirit and break bread with his enemy. Then he remembered how he had been the enemy of God and God forgave him. So in his heart he forgave that man and walked back, sat down, and broke the bread with that brother. This is what it is. How can you break bread if you still have an unforgiving spirit towards your brother or your sister? How can you break bread if there is something unsettled between you and the Lord? You cannot come with an evil conscience. Prove yourself; then this breaking of bread will really be meaningful, powerful, exalting, and building up.

Come With Our Baskets Full

In Deuteronomy 16:16 the children of Israel were commanded to go to Jerusalem to the feasts three times a year—Passover, Pentecost, and Feast of Tabernacles. And God said, "Whenever you go to a feast you should not go empty-handed." In Deuteronomy 26:2 it says, "Bring all the produce of the first fruits; put them in the basket and bring it to the Lord. Lay that basket by the altar." In other words, when we come to the Lord's table, can we come empty-handed? No. We should come with our basket full. But if we do not till the ground during that time, we have nothing to offer. So in our daily life, how we need to cultivate our life with the Lord! In our daily life we experience His mercy, His forgiveness, His love, His longsuffering, His faithfulness, His supply, His protection, and His keeping. If we live a life with Him during the week, our basket will be full. We cannot come empty-handed, and as a result we will have to offer the sacrifice of praise to Him. It is not a law, a rule, or legalistic. Some may have been at the Lord's table for years, yet have never opened their mouth to say, "Thank You." Can you do that? Is that a worthy manner? Why do you hold back? Is it because you have nothing to offer? Or is it because you cannot pray and praise as beautiful or as eloquent as some brothers and sisters? What pleases the Lord? It is the heart, and it may just be a word. Do not hide yourself under hymns or choruses as a substitute, but bring your personal offering to the Lord. The breaking of bread should be a time that the Lord will be so honored, so worshiped, and so praised, that when He looks upon us it will be as Isaiah says, "And His heart shall be satisfied." I wonder how satisfied the heart of our Lord is at our Lord's table. Are we gathering together for worse or are we gathering together for better? May the Lord have mercy on us. I speak to myself, and I want to share it with you brothers and sisters. The breaking of bread is the holiest time of the church life. Never miss it. It is so important, and it is our very life. The more we know it, the more we realize how much it means not only to us but to our Lord. God bless us.

8—Spiritual Gifts

I Corinthians 12:31—But desire earnestly the greater gifts, and yet shew I unto you a way of more surpassing excellence.

We have all been called into the fellowship of God's Son Jesus Christ, and I do hope that every one of us will really realize what an honor, what a glory, and what measureless love is behind this. God and our Lord Jesus have opened up their fellowship to us in order that we may share the same with our Lord Jesus and with our heavenly Father, our God. No one can measure the riches of that fellowship, and because it is so precious, therefore anything that is contradictory to that fellowship has to be dealt with. That is the them of I Corinthians. The Corinthian believers were the Lord's. They were saved, but unfortunately, they still wanted to continue on with their old lives, and it was a contradiction. So by the grace of God, He will deliver us from such a situation.

The last six chapters of I Corinthians are concerned with this matter of church life. Church life is fellowship life and body life. And in this body life, there are a number of things that are very essential. In Acts 2:42, we are told that those who believed in the Lord Jesus, whether they had believed in the Lord for years or were new believers, would continue in the teaching and the fellowship of the apostles, which was none other than the teaching and the fellowship of Christ. And the two things that express this obedience to the fellowship and teaching of our Lord are the breaking of bread and prayers. The breaking of bread is a corporate thing. You cannot break the bread and remember the Lord all by yourself. You need at least two. So it is a corporate expression. And so is the prayer. We may have our private prayer, personal prayer, and we should; but more than that, we should come together and pray together in corporate prayer. Now, these are the two most essential and practical ways of expressing our body life, fellowship life, or church life.

The Spirituals

There are a number of things in these six chapters that we could share on, but the Corinthian believers wrote to the apostle Paul about certain things, and one of the things they wrote to him about was concerning the spirituals. The heading on chapter 12 is "But Concerning Spirituals," which is the original phrase, and is explained as spiritual manifestations or spiritual gifts.

Paul said to the Corinthian believers in the first chapter: "You are rich in words and knowledge." They were very rich in doctrine and in teaching. They were also very rich in knowledge—not only worldly knowledge but even knowledge of the word of God. Not only that, Paul said, "You are short in no gift." The Corinthian church was very gifted. Naturally, Corinth was famous for its eloquence, and even in the church, they were rich in words and knowledge, and they were not short in gifts; they were a very gifted assembly. You would think that an assembly that is rich in words and knowledge and is not short of any gift would be a tremendous, wonderful assembly. But on the contrary, in spite of all their endowments, their lives were corrupt, and they abused the gifts that God had given to them.

So the Corinthian church wrote to Paul asking him about spiritual gifts. They were not asking about whether they had gifts or not because they had many gifts. But because of these gifts, a lot of confusion had come into their midst. Therefore, it was not a matter of whether they had gifts or not but how to exercise their gifts. Gifts are given for the sake of the building of the church, the body of Christ. But whenever gifts are separated from the body, and they become a personal thing instead of a corporate thing, there are bound to be problems. You cannot separate gifts from the body because spiritual gifts are given for the building of the body of Christ. Even today, there is a lot of confusion among God's people about this matter of spiritual gifts. So I think it is very timely that we should really go into these chapters 12-14. They will give us some basic understanding that will help us from being confused and also help us to exercise our gifts in the way that God has purposed for them.

Natural Talents

What are spiritual gifts? I think if we want to understand this, we have to go back to when God created man. God gave gifts to man. When we are born, God has already endowed us with natural talents. Otherwise, how can we live? How can we live in a society in which God has purposed that we live together? If a person is born without natural endowment, without any ability given to him, without any natural talents, he will not be able to live. He will not be able to behave and fulfill his responsibility in society. In other words, everyone that is born into this world has been gifted by God with natural talents. And they are all different because God loves variety, and when you put them all together, it is fullness. Now that is how it is with natural talents.

After we are born again from above, and we are in the house of God or the family of God, God will give us spiritual gifts so that we may know how to behave among God's people and build up one another. There is a difference between natural talents and spiritual gifts. Sometimes it seems that natural talents and spiritual gifts coincide, but at other times a spiritual gift can be just the opposite of your natural talent. But whether they are together or not, one thing is certain, according to the word of God, natural talents are for living in the world, and spiritual gifts are given that we may live in the spiritual world—that is, the church, the assembly, the fellowship, or the body of Christ. They are two different things working in two different areas.

Mixing Up Natural and Spiritual

The problem comes among God's people when they mix up natural talents and spiritual gifts, which is very common in Christianity. If you are naturally endowed with an executive talent, then in the world, you can be an executive. After you are saved, in Christianity they say, "You have natural talent because you are an executive; come and be an elder in the church, so that you can use your talent to serve God." Naturally, you are very musical, and after you are saved they want you to use your talent to serve God. That is the exhortation we find in Christianity, but it is totally against God's word.

Moses, for instance, was endowed with natural talents. Not only that, God seemed to arrange his environment to develop his natural talents. He was "mighty in words and in deeds." Moses had a heart for God. He knew that God had a purpose in his life, so he wanted to use his natural talents to accomplish God's purpose. He tried to save his people with his "mighty in words and mighty in deeds." You remember how he killed an Egyptian to save the Hebrews and how he used his eloquence to try to decide the struggle between two Hebrew brothers. But God allowed him to be a total failure. What if he had succeeded? Then the children of Israel would never have left Egypt, and probably they would have taken over Egypt. So God allowed him to fail completely. He had to spend forty years in the wilderness to unlearn everything that he had naturally learned until he could not speak. After you speak to a few sheep for forty years, you lose your eloquence. He said, "Who am I to go to face Pharaoh, the king? I am nothing." He was eighty years old when he wrote in Psalm 90: "A man lives in this world usually seventy years, but if you are strong, you may live eighty years." He was eighty years old at that time and at the end of his natural life. Then God appeared to him and said: "I am with you. I will be your eloquence. I will be your ability." The Spirit of God came upon him, and he was able to fulfill God's work.

So it does not mean that God will totally discard your natural talent because if you read the story of Moses, you find that for a person to lead a million people forty years in the wilderness requires some ability. God can use it, but it has to go through death and be resurrected. In other words, it should not be in your hand anymore but in the hand of God. So let us remember that there is a tremendous difference—a difference of heaven and earth—between natural talent and spiritual gift. Sometimes God does the opposite, but when they seem to work together, as history shows us, it always has to go through death and resurrection. All our natural talents have to go through death before God can pick them up and use them.

Spiritual Gifts for the Body of Christ

Spiritual gifts are given for the purpose that we may live and function in the body of Christ. They are never given for personal reasons. This is where the Corinthian believers made a big mistake because they took spiritual gifts for their personal use. And the gift they sought most was speaking in tongues because it was miraculous and could easily put them on display. So they had a misunderstanding as to spiritual gifts. That is the reason why in I Corinthians 12, Paul said, "Concerning the spirituals." They were asking Paul: "How can we be spiritual? How can we prove we are spiritual? If we speak in tongues, surely that is being spiritual because it is not natural." So they were mixed up about speaking in tongues as *the* sign of being spiritual. And even today, we see the same error among God's people.

This is the reason Paul had to remind them: "Before you believed in the Lord, you worshiped idols, you worshiped demons, and you had your so-called spiritual experience." Now it is entirely different. You are in the Holy Spirit—not the evil spirit, and there is a tremendous difference. If you are in the Holy Spirit, you will say, "Jesus is Lord." If you cannot say, "Jesus is Lord" in the Spirit, that is the evil spirit, and that is the way to test the spirit. We find out that when the spirit is tested in that way, it works because, if it is a demon possession or an evil possession, he will never recognize Jesus as Lord. But remember, you have to address the spirit and not the person because the person may be a believer, and he will say, "Jesus is Lord." But if you hold onto the spirit, then the spirit will refuse to say, "Jesus is Lord." This is always true. So it does not mean that if you speak in tongues you become spiritual instantly. Not at all!

Spiritual gifts are given because we are in the body of Christ. So when Paul mentioned spiritual gifts in I Corinthians 12, he immediately connected them with the body. "The body is one, but there are many members; many members but one body, so also is the Christ" (see v. 12). That is the body of Christ. We need to remember that whenever we speak of spiritual gifts, it has to be related to the body because even though they are given to individuals, they are members of the body of Christ. They are given because we are members of the body, and being in the body, we have a function to fulfill. And how can we fulfill that function as members of the body of Christ? We fulfill it by the spiritual gifts we have received.

The Natural Body

We have different members that make up our natural body. We have hands, feet, inner organs, and many outward organs. We have various members in our body, and none of them lives for itself. All the members of our physical body live for the body. The eye cannot say to the ear, "I do not need you." Nor can the ear say to the eye, "Because I am not an eye I am not of the body." All the members of the body are different, and it is God who has arranged it. It is God who has given us this body, and it is His will to include all the different members in it.

It is the same way in the body of Christ. There are many members—much more than in the physical body—but not all the members are the same. All the members of the body are different. Some may be like hands or feet or the mouth or the ear, because if it is all one member, where is the body? So we need to remember that we are members of the one body of Christ, and not only members, but we are different members and members in particular. This is not our choice but God's arrangement. God put us in the body of Christ, and wherever He puts us is the best place. We are not to admire other people but to be faithful in what God has given us.

So we can see that the purpose of a spiritual gift is just like the purpose of natural talent. The purpose of natural talent is for our body to live and function properly that we may grow. And the purpose of a spiritual gift is exactly the same, but it is in a different area. It is in the spiritual body of Christ, and we all are "members one of another."

When do we receive spiritual gifts? This has become a very confusing issue among God's people today. Some say that you receive spiritual gifts when you receive the baptism with the Holy Spirit. Others say that you receive spiritual gifts when people lay hands upon you. Some others say you receive them when you are born again. And still, others say that you cannot know if you have spiritual gifts unless you speak in tongues. They believe speaking in tongues is *the* gift, *the* sign of baptism with the Holy Spirit.

There are all kinds of confusing ideas, but God's word is always very simple. Men make everything complicated, but if we remember how God gives us natural talents, then it solves the whole problem.

When a baby is born, God has so arranged that the baby has eyes, a nose, a mouth, ears, hands, feet, and inner organs. Every member of our natural body has been given to us, and when we are born, every organ in our body, every member in our body, has already been endowed by God with a natural talent. He gives us eyes, and can God give us eyes and not give us the gift of seeing? That is what the eye is for. He gives us ears, and can you believe that He makes the ear for any other reason than to hear? Then what is the use of the ear? Therefore, when we come out of the womb of our mother, all the organs are there, and all the gifts are there.

But a baby who has just been born cannot see; he has eyes but cannot see. The baby has hands, but he cannot handle. The baby has feet, but he cannot walk. However, as long as the baby has life, all these things will come as he grows. In a few days, he begins to see. He cannot walk in the beginning, and he thinks he has to walk on his hands and feet together, so he crawls. Gradually, he discovers if he does not use his hands to help, he can walk better—so why use the hands? He has a mouth, but he cannot eat solid food. He can only drink milk from the mother but, gradually, through exercise, he is able to take solid food. He cannot speak but, after a while, he finds he can utter sounds and then words.

Now I would like to ask a question. Is the gift of seeing given when you can see? No, it was given when you were born, but it was dormant. It needs life in order to grow, and then all these gifts will be manifested. And the more you exercise your gift, the better it will be—for instance, the eyes. Some people can see things in the dark. Why? It is through exercise; it is that simple.

The Spiritual Body

It is the same rule in the body of Christ. When do we receive the baptism with the Holy Spirit? We receive the baptism with the Holy Spirit when we are born again. When we are born into the family of God, the Bible tells us that we are born of the Spirit. He that is born of the Spirit is spirit—that is new birth. When the Holy Spirit begets us, and we are born of the Holy Spirit, our dead spirit—dead in sins and transgression—was raised into life. We have a new spirit, and we cry out to God, "Abba, Father."

More than that, we are not just born from above; we are born into the family of God. When are we born into the family of God? It is at our new birth. So whenever we are born again, we are immediately born into the family of God. And that can be easily proven because when we meet another brother or sister and realize that he or she is also a brother or sister in the Lord, immediately there is a bond. And that bond is stronger than the natural bond with our natural brothers and sisters. This is the baptism with the Holy Spirit.

The Baptism with the Holy Spirit

What is the meaning of the baptism with the Holy Spirit? It is not the sight or the sound; it is being born into the family of God. So in I Corinthians 12:13 it says, "For also in one Spirit you were baptized into one body, whether Jews or Greeks, whether bondmen or freemen, and all have been given to drink of one Spirit." That is the meaning of the baptism with the Holy Spirit. We are baptized in one Spirit into one body. We, who are born again, are baptized into the body of Christ. The Holy Spirit not only begets us with a new spirit, but He also comes and dwells in our new spirit and becomes our Comforter and our Parakletos. He is with us. He never leaves us. He teaches us, He directs us, He transforms us and conforms us to Christ Jesus.

At the same time, He has put us in the family of God. That is what happened when you were born again. Can you be born again and not be given the corresponding spiritual gifts? Otherwise, God's work is incomplete. How can He put me in the body of Christ as a member and not give me any gift to fulfill my function? Unthinkable! So, according to God's word, our spiritual gift has already been given when we were born again and brought into the body of Christ. The spiritual gifts are already there.

God never does a work halfway. Whenever He works, it is fully done. Today, I think lots of brothers and sisters are confused. They ask, "What is my spiritual gift? Can you tell me what my spiritual gift is?" Do you need anyone to tell you what your spiritual gift is? You should know. Why don't you know? There is a reason. You do not grow. If your life does not grow, your spiritual gift will not be manifested and will be dormant forever. Therefore, we have a responsibility. We do not need to ask what our spiritual gift is. On the other hand, we need to ask ourselves if we are growing in the Lord.

After you are saved, if you really follow the leading of the Holy Spirit in you, somehow as you grow, the Lord will impress upon you something. Or, to put it another way, He will burden you with something that is related to your brothers and sisters or to the house of God. Other people may not notice, but you notice it, and that is your calling. God is calling you to fulfill your function in this area.

Spiritual Gifts are for Service

Spiritual gifts are given for service. We are not born into the family of God just to be a burden to our brothers and sisters in the church family. We are born into the family of God to be a contributor. Every member is to function and to contribute something to the welfare of the building up of the body of Christ. In other words, we are not born again for our selfish reason. We are born again for God and for God's house. Otherwise, why should we be born again? We are born to serve. "Let My people go that they may serve Me" (see Exodus 8:1). We are not to serve our own purpose anymore. We are to serve the purpose of God, and the purpose of God is the building of His house unto the full growth of the body of Christ. That is God's purpose, and that is why spiritual gifts are given.

If you really have a heart for God, when you are among God's people, supernaturally naturally, He will burden you with something, and that is the direction He is guiding you. Do it for the Lord. And as you begin to do it, you will find God's blessing follows, not only in you but in your brothers and sisters. And if God's blessing follows, go further. That is how your gifts are developed, and that is how your gifts are exercised. Unfortunately, today some of God's people are saved just for themselves and not for God or for the house of God. As a result of this, their gifts are buried. That is the way to bury it. Every servant of God is given talents—some have five talents, some two talents, and some have one talent, but all are given at least one talent (see Matthew 25:14-30). The problem is: do you trade with it, or do you bury it? The exhortation is: be faithful.

You know why you need a so-called experience of baptism with the Holy Spirit in order to have that gift released? It is because in your daily life, you do not live a consecrated life. You do not live a life for the Lord. Therefore, you need a special time of reviving so that what has been dormant can be released. From time to time, you need a revival, and when revival comes, it seems as if your gift is manifested, and when you are getting low before the Lord, that gift is buried again, and you need another revival to stir you up. That should not be the case.

In Romans 12, it is very true that consecration is related to functioning because after you are consecrated, you present your body a living sacrifice, then you realize you are in the body, and you begin to function. So the reason most believers are not functioning in the body of Christ is that they are not growing in the Lord. Seek the Lord, give yourself to the Lord, allow the Spirit to work in you so that gift in you that is dormant may be manifested, and never isolate it from the body of Christ.

Exercising Spiritual Gifts

How should our spiritual gifts be exercised? The Corinthian believers had lots of gifts. They were not short in gifts, but because there were too many gifts, the body was not built; it was being destroyed. So the apostle Paul said, "Good, you have gifts, but do you know how to exercise them? I will show you a more surpassing, excellent way." The apostle Paul had to use not double but triple emphasis. You say, "Excellence should be enough, an excellent way." No, he said, "A more surpassing, excellent way." So that must be pretty excellent. And what is the excellent way?

I Corinthians 12 is on the body and the gifts in the members of the body. Chapter 14 is the exercising of the gifts in the body, but chapter 13 is the more excellent way. What is the more excellent way? It is love, but not what we usually call love. It is the love that only comes from God, the love of Christ, the agape love. It is the love that comes with the life He gave us.

In other words, if you want to make the distinction, love is grace. Grace is for life; gift is for service. Gift is power, but that power needs to be handled with care and with the right life. If you give a knife to a little child, his life is not mature enough to handle that knife. He may hurt people and hurt himself, but the knife in the hand of a grown-up is so useful.

All the confusion that is found in Christianity today is because the emphasis is on gift and not on life. God gives us life (which is grace), and God means for this life to handle the gift. If life is immature, the greater the gift is, the more disastrous it becomes. Unfortunately, we find this everywhere because there is not a corresponding life to use the gift.

The Person and Manifestation of the Holy Spirit

The tremendous error among God's people is that they cannot test the spirit. The Bible tells us that there is a great difference between the Person of the Holy Spirit and the manifestations of the Holy Spirit. The Person of the Holy Spirit is divine. He is God. The manifestation of the Holy

Spirit in gifts is not personal. We need to obey the Person of the Holy Spirit. In Acts 5:32, it says God gives the Holy Spirit to those who obey Him. We need to obey the Holy Spirit. The Holy Spirit who dwells in us is God, is divine, and He is the Person. We need to honor Him and not grieve Him nor quench Him. We should obey Him. But the gift is His manifestation and not His Person.

So far as gifts are concerned, they need to be handled or controlled by the one who has the gifts. In I Corinthians 14:32, it says, "The spirits of the prophets are subject to the prophets." In other words, the ones who are gifted are supposed to handle this gift and not be handled by it. So when people think they are receiving the baptism, they dare not test the spirit because they think they will be dishonoring the Holy Spirit. Not so! The gift has to be handled by you. The spirits of the prophets obey the spirit. You can manage it.

Sometimes, when people speak in tongues, they dare not stop. Or they speak it in a wrong situation, just like the Bible says: "In a gathering, you speak in tongues, but there is no interpreter." The word says, "If there is no interpreter, speak to yourself. Be silent." But in our experience, people think because they are in the spirit, they have to allow the spirit to continue; there is no control. That is absolutely wrong! We have gone through this and suffered for it.

Manifestations are impersonal; therefore, those who are gifted need to handle them, control them, use them wisely, comelily, and orderly. If only we can see the difference, I think that will help us from falling into all kinds of confusion.

But the question will be asked: "Doesn't it say in I Corinthians 12:31, "Desire earnestly the greater gifts"? Then in chapter 14:1, it says, "Follow after love, and be emulous of spiritual manifestations, but rather that ye may prophesy." We know that spiritual gifts are given by the Holy Spirit, as we find in chapter 12:11: "But all these things operates the one and the same Spirit, dividing to each in particular according as he pleases."

It pleases the Holy Spirit to give this person a word of knowledge, to give that member a word of wisdom, to give this one prophecy, to give the other one tongues, and the other one interpretation. It is according to the desire of the Holy Spirit. We do not choose. Then why is it that it says, "Desire earnestly the greater gifts, emulous of spiritual manifestations, but rather that ye may prophesy," as if we could do that? Is that a contradiction? Not at all! Spiritual gifts can be increased. The one with five talents earned five more, the one with two talents earned two more, but if the one with one talent is not trading, it is buried and remains as one talent. That is the problem. If we are truly faithful to what the Spirit of God has apportioned us, our talents or spiritual gifts will increase because we are no longer babes. A babe seeks only for his display, but when he grows up, and his mind is growing, he is thinking of others and thinking especially of the body of Christ. He is thinking about how to help, how to contribute, and because his mind has been transformed, and he is growing in the Lord. Therefore God will give him greater gifts so he can serve in a greater way. Isn't it strange when people whose eyes are blind, their other senses seem to be keener and take up some of the function of the eyes? Isn't that wonderful!

I recently heard of a blind person who could see color with his ear. When people described the color to him, somehow, he could see it. Spiritual gifts can be developed and increased to the glory of God, but remember, they are not for our sake. All the gifts are for the edification of the body of Christ. They are not "headification" as brother Sparks would say, but edification. All gifts are for the building of the body of Christ. So there is no contradiction. People may speak in tongues, but in the assembly, it is much better to speak five words with intelligence than ten thousand words in tongues because it is for the building of the body of Christ.

How we need to be delivered from making gifts a personal thing! Gifts are not for ourselves but for the building up of the body of Christ. And all gifts need to be exercised by the life of Christ in us, and if the life of Christ is in control, everything will be done comelily and in an orderly manner.

These are very basic, and I hope that we can have the right understanding concerning spiritual gifts.

9—Overcoming Deception

I Corinthians 15:58—So then, my beloved brethren, be firm, immovable, abounding always in the work of the Lord, knowing that your toil is not in vain in the Lord.

This letter to the Corinthian believers is always considered a very negative letter because the church in Corinth had so many problems. Many of these problems they knew about. But with some of the problems, they were not conscious of them or that they were so serious. But thank God, He is always positive, so His servant Paul, in writing this letter to the Corinthian believers, always took a positive step throughout this letter. He began with this declaration: "God is faithful, who has called us into the fellowship of His Son Jesus Christ."

Can any statement be more positive than this one? God is faithful. He has called us into the fellowship of His Son Jesus Christ. There is nothing that is more glorious than this calling. Think of that! We are called by God into this fellowship that He and His Son have had even from eternity past. What a fellowship that must be! How rich it must be! How harmonious! The fellowship of the Father with His Son and the fellowship of the Son with His Father is perfect, abundant, and spiritual. They are sharing equally together. They are the same; they are one—and yet this fellowship has been extended to us—even us. The very thought of that overwhelms me. We are called to come and enter in and to have a share even in this glorious fellowship. We are called to know Him in His fullness, in His purpose, in His heart, in

His desire, in His way, and to have such fellowship with one another. Just as the apostle John said, "Our fellowship is with the Father and the Son, and what we have known we report to you, that you may have fellowship with us, that our heart may be full of joy."

How precious is this calling! Have we really responded to that calling? Is it not true that there are many problems and many things that will be contradictory, that will oppose, resist, and destroy this wonderful fellowship? And there is nothing more destructive than what the Corinthian believers had committed, and that is carnality. Even though they were saved by the grace of God and had received the life of Christ from above, which is pure, perfect, spiritual, and heavenly, they still continued to live by their natural life, their self-life or their flesh, instead of living by the life of Christ. And this became the greatest hindrance to the fellowship.

Paul was trying to help them see so they could get out of this state and enter into this wonderful fellowship. The secret, of course, is Jesus Christ and Him crucified. If only they could see what the Lord Jesus had done for them on the cross, if only they would allow the cross to work in their lives, then they would be delivered from their carnality and truly enjoy that sweet fellowship with Christ, with the Father, and with one another. That describes the first Corinthian letter.

We have shared together a number of times on I Corinthians, and when you come to the end of chapter 14, it says, "But let all things be done comelily and with order." Paul was dealing with this matter of spiritual gifts, how to exercise these gifts, how we should meet together, and he said, "Let all things be done comelily, beautifully, harmoniously, peacefully, and with divine order—no confusion, no mistake."

It seems to me that this word is the end of this letter. If everything is done comelily and orderly, then what more can be said? But when Paul was coming to the conclusion of his letter, he remembered there was something else just as important that he needed to say. So there are two more chapters added.

Resurrection

Chapter 15 is a chapter on resurrection. Paul discovered among the believers in Corinth that there were some who said, "There is no such thing as resurrection." Even at the time of our Lord Jesus, the Sadducees, who were the leading party in Judaism at that time in the priesthood, did not believe in the resurrection. From their human reasoning, resurrection seemed to be out of the question. There is no such thing! But to Paul, not believing in resurrection struck at the very heart of the gospel of Jesus Christ. He said, "But I make known to you, brethren, the glad tidings [the gospel] which I announced to you, which also ye received, in which also ye stand, by which also ye are saved."

This is the gospel of Jesus Christ that Paul received from the Lord and delivered to the Corinthian believers. They received it, they stood on it, and they were saved by it. That is the very foundation, and yet there were some who did not believe in resurrection. So in dealing with this matter, the apostle Paul again took a positive stand, and he reiterated the gospel. He said, "For I delivered to you, in the first place, what also I had received. That is what I received from the Lord by revelation, that Christ died for our sins, according to the Scriptures; and that he was buried; and that he was raised the third day, according to the scriptures; and that he appeared to Cephas, then to the twelve. Then he appeared to about five hundred brethren at once, of whom the most remain until now, but some also have fallen asleep. Then he appeared to James; then to all the apostles; and last of all, as to an abortion, he appeared to me also" (I Corinthians 15:3-8).

In other words, what are the chief articles of faith in the gospel? What is the gospel? The gospel is that Christ Jesus died for our sins. He was buried, but He was raised from the dead and appeared alive to many who are His. That is our belief, and that is our faith. If anyone does not believe in resurrection, it means that he did not really receive the gospel according to what is written in the word of God. It is against the very truth of God. Anything that is added to the gospel, as revealed in the Scriptures, or anything that is taken away from the Scriptures is a serious thing because God shall take away his part from the tree of life (see Revelation 22:18-19). There is no eternal life if anyone does not believe what the Bible says or adds more to the Bible.

False Teaching on Resurrection

The apostle Paul tells us in this chapter that if anyone does not believe in resurrection then everything is vain—what we say is vain. We become false witnesses. What you receive is vain because it does not work any longer, so you are still in sin. Even though you say you believe in the Lord Jesus, if you reject resurrection then our Lord Jesus has not been raised from the dead, and your faith is vain. It does not work, and you are still in sin. Nothing has happened. Worse than that, we become false witnesses. And the apostle said, "If believing in the Lord Jesus is just for this life, then we are the most miserable of all men because if you really follow the Lord you have to pay a cost, you have to suffer, and if there is no life after death, then why are you doing it? You are the most miserable people in the whole world." There is a direct connection between truth and life. In other words, it says, "Evil communications corrupt good manners" (v. 33). What you believe will result in how you live.

"Evil communications corrupt good manners." You cannot divide these two things. Truth will give you the right kind of life, but anything that is a falsehood will lead you astray, and you will corrupt your life. That is for sure. So it is extremely important that we believe whatever is in the Scriptures. Never add anything to it nor take away anything from it.

In Isaiah 8:20, it says, "To the law and to the testimony!" Everything is to be judged by what the word says.

The Order of Resurrection

So in this chapter, Paul not only reiterates the cardinal articles of faith in the gospel, but he also tries to explain to them a certain measure of the order of resurrection. Christ will be raised first as the first fruits, and then we who believe in Him will also be raised. Some people have asked: "If there is resurrection, what kind of body will we have?" So Paul tried to explain that it is like a seed you plant, and as the seed grows, it takes on a body that God has given it. Everything has its own body. You plant a mortal body, but in the resurrection it is an immortal body. What you plant is a natural body but what comes out in resurrection is a spiritual body. Then he also tells us that when the resurrection happens, it is in the twinkling of an eye. At the sound of the last trumpet and the shout of the archangels, those who are asleep in Christ will be raised first. Then those who are still living on the earth will be changed, and all will be caught up to meet the Lord in the air. So this is a great chapter on resurrection, telling us what is resurrection, when it will happen, how it happens, and what will happen. That is according to the Scriptures.

God's Truth Has Always Been Challenged

Now we would like to enlarge this to cover all kinds of false teaching because any teaching that is not according to the Scriptures, or any teaching that adds to or takes away anything from what the Scriptures say is a heresy, and this is a very serious matter. Even from the beginning of human history God's truth was challenged. In the garden of Eden, God said, "You can eat of all the trees in the garden except the tree of the knowledge of good and evil, because if you eat it you shall die." Even the one in the midst of the garden—the Tree of Life—was not forbidden. That is God's word, and that is the truth. But Satan tempted Eve and questioned God's word by adding so much more to it. He said, "Did God say you cannot eat any tree?" Now if Adam and Eve were forbidden to eat any tree then they would die because they would have no food. Eve said, "No, God did not say that." God said, "We cannot eat that tree nor touch it." Now something was added. God never said, "You cannot touch it."

So when you try to add or take away anything from God's word, it is heresy and false teaching. What is the result of false teaching? Adam and Eve lost their glory and discovered that they were naked. They hid themselves among the trees from the presence of God because they could not face God anymore. But thank God, He was merciful. He prepared a salvation for them and clothed them with the skin of a slain animal; but they were driven out of the garden of Eden.

So, wherever there is truth there will be falsehood. Or we can put it in reverse. If there is falsehood there must be truth also; otherwise where will be the counterfeit? If you find a counterfeit currency, maybe a fifty or hundred dollar bill, you know there must be the true or the real currency. But false currency cannot be used. Not only is it useless, it is a crime.

From the very beginning of the history of mankind and throughout human history, especially among God's people, whether it was with the children of Israel in the past or with the church of God today, there have been false teachers, false prophets, heresy, and heretic teachings. That is the reason why we need to be careful.

New Testament False Teachings

When you read all the letters in the New Testament, from Romans to Revelation, you find that even in the first century in all these letters there is the mention of false teaching. For instance, in Romans, which is a full dissertation on the gospel of Jesus Christ, there is the mention of false teaching in chapter 6. Paul said, "There is someone who says let us continue to sin that grace may abound." Now what kind of teaching is that? You can continue to sin, because the more you sin the more abundant will be grace. Paul said, "God forbid!" That is a false teaching. We who believe in the Lord Jesus should not commit sin. Thank God, even if we slip and sin there is a provision for us. That is the mercy of God, but we should not continue to sin as if grace will always be there.

I Corinthians is, of course, full of examples of false teaching and corrupt living everywhere.

In Galatians there is "another gospel" being preached because they had added law into grace. Believing in the Lord Jesus was not enough—they had to keep the Law and be circumcised. Now what kind of teaching is that added to the gospel? And Paul said, "That is another gospel."

In Ephesians you could say that everything is very positive. There is nothing negative in it; that is true. But even in Ephesians they had to learn to put off that which is of the old and to put on that which is of the new. So there is still the danger that we may continue to live according to the flesh and not according to the spirit.

In Colossians they loved the Lord, they sought the Lord, and yet they were told they would not be complete. They wanted perfection but the teaching was that they could not arrive at perfection unless they believed in the mystic teachings and practiced certain rituals.

In I Thessalonians there were some who said that resurrection had passed; therefore, those who were still living and believed in the Lord Jesus had no hope. And II Thessalonians said, "The day of the Lord, which is the judgment of God, has already come, so you are too late. What kind of teaching is that?

In Timothy, Titus, Hebrews, Philemon and all the rest, it seems as if there were always mentions of false teachings and false prophets, and that is why when you come to the later epistles there is always that warning. For instance, the apostle Paul tells us in his second letter to Timothy that we are living in the last days, and in the last days there will be false teachers. People will be lovers of self, pleasure, and the world rather than lovers of God and lovers of truth. These are dangerous days, and we need to be very careful.

The apostle Peter in II Peter says it is the end of the days, and in those days there will be mockers.

In I, II, III John he says, "Little children, we are in the last hour. The spirit of antichrist is everywhere." In I John there is mention of a false teaching: "Do not believe in the deity of the Lord Jesus but say that He is just a man. Reject Him as the Son to the Father." In II John it is just the reverse. There is reference to a false teaching that denies Christ has come to be a man. It denies His humanity. And of course in III John we find the result of it, that Diotrephes became such a tyrant in the church.

In Jude it says, "I am going to write to you about our faith and then I feel I have to contend for it because people even deny the Master, our Lord."

The Candidates of False Teaching

So if this is true at the end of the apostolic age, how much more real is it today! Thank God He is working everywhere. The gospel is preached all over the world, but at the same time, wherever the gospel is preached, whenever the Lord is working, Satan is also working. False teachings, false prophets, false messiahs, and Christs are everywhere. Especially as we are coming to the end of this age, all these things are increasing greatly. Many will be deceived, and again and again, the word of God warns us to be vigilant, to be careful, to take heed, and do not go to sleep.

How are we going to face such situations? When we are surrounded with all these things, the number one thing is this. If a lie is a black lie, as it were, if it is all lie, if there is no truth in it, nobody will believe it. But if it is a white lie, if there is some truth in it and yet it is mixed with lots of untruth, that is the thing that can deceive us. I feel that as long as we live in this world we can never be so confident of ourselves that we will never be deceived. If you ever think you are beyond deception, you are already in deep deception. The apostle Paul says, "I do not trust in the flesh." Once we trust in our flesh, thinking that we will not be deceived, that we are so knowledgeable and know everything, and we are so spiritual, then we are the ones who will fall into deception. We are the candidates for false teaching. Never trust in yourself, no matter how spiritual you are, no matter how long you have believed in the Lord, no matter how knowledgeable you think you are. The danger is that once we lose our watchfulness, the enemy will come in. So we are never to trust in ourselves.

Now if you do not trust yourself, then who can you trust? Trust the Lord! There is One who is trustworthy. Do not trust in any man no matter how spiritual that man is. Trust the Lord! The apostle Paul says, "I know whom I have believed, and I know that He is able to keep that which I have committed to Him." Commit yourself to the Lord. He is the only One who is able to keep you from falling. Seek the Lord, put your trust in the Lord and humble yourself before the Lord. Never take the position that you are above deception. Humbly commit yourself to the Lord, and the Lord is able to keep you to the very end.

Provisions to Keep Us From Falling

Thank God, He has given us some provisions to keep us from falling into deception. As a matter of fact, if we really listen to what the word of God says, even a babe in Christ will not be deceived. Oftentimes, those who seem to be more knowledgeable and more spiritual fall into false teachings faster and easier than those who are babes in Christ and newly born. Why?

In I John 2:18 he says, "Little children, it is the last hour, and, according as ye have heard that antichrist comes, even now there have come many antichrists, whence we know that it is the last hour."

Vv. 20-25: "And ye have the unction, the anointing from the holy one, and ye know all things. I have not written to you because ye do not know the truth, but because ye know it, and that no lie is of the truth. Who is the liar but he who denies that Jesus is the Christ? He is the antichrist who denies the Father and the Son. Whoever denies the Son has not the Father either; he who confesses the Son has the Father also. As for you let that which ye have heard from the beginning abide in you: if what ye have heard from the beginning abides in you, ye also shall abide in the Son and in the Father. And this is the promise which he has promised us, life eternal."

The Holy Spirit

God has provided two most important provisions. Number one is His Spirit. Everyone who believes in the Lord Jesus, even the newly born child of God, has the Holy Spirit of God living in him. He is the holy anointing. He is the One who keeps you in Christ Jesus. He is the One who teaches you in all things—big things and small things. He is the One who will tell you what is true, what is untrue, what is of God, and what is not of God. The Holy Spirit who lives within you will teach you in all things.

In the Old Covenant the Holy Spirit had not yet dwelt in human hearts. Therefore, if you wanted to know any truth, you had to be taught because the Law was written outside; it was not written upon the heart. You had to be taught to know the Law. But in the New Covenant we do not need anyone to teach us because we have a Teacher within. He will teach us in all things, and we will know Him inwardly. If it is not the Spirit, we will know. How do we know? We just know (see I John 2:18-27).

I knew a brother who was newly saved, and he went to Boston. I was in New York at that time. He did not know much about the Bible, but when he went to Boston, he heard a teaching. And when he heard it, he sensed in his heart that it was not true. He did not know how to refute it because he did not have the knowledge, but inwardly, he knew it was not right. When he came back, he talked with me about it, and sure enough it was a false teaching. It concerned the deity of our Lord Jesus.

After we are saved and we are walking in this inner way of life, depending upon the Spirit of God who lives within us and not upon what people say to us, listening to the inner voice, we will be delivered from many falsehoods. Unfortunately, most Christians do not do that. When the Holy Spirit moves within us, we neglect it. We hear so many voices that we do not have the quietness to hear what the Spirit says. But the Lord has made provision for even a child or a babe in Christ to deliver him from anything that is outside of the truth if only he will listen. The anointing that we received from Him abides in us, and we have no need that anyone should teach us. "But as the same unction teaches you as to all things, and is true and is not a lie, and even as it has taught you, ye shall abide in him" (I John 2:27b).

The Word of God

Then we have another provision of the Lord: "What you have heard from the beginning" (see I John 1:1). That is the Scripture, the word of God. We have the Holy Spirit within us, and we have the word of God before us. And these two agree because every Scripture is God-breathed (see II Timothy 3:16-17). It is profitable for teaching, conviction, correction, and instruction. That is why we need to study the word of God carefully—not carelessly but carefully—because the word of God or the truth will tell us what is true and what is untrue. If we hear something that is added to the word of God or we hear something that takes away from the word of God, be careful. This is untrue. So God has given these two ready provisions to keep us from falling.

The Body of Christ

Then I will add another one to it, and that is the protection of the body of Christ. As an individual, we cannot live all by ourselves. God saved us individually, but He saved us in order to bring us into the family of God and become a member of the body of Christ. It is not God's will that we who are saved should live alone.

As we learn to live with our brothers and sisters, we will meet many crosses. Do not think that the cross you meet comes only from the world. More crosses come from the church. If we really live church life and body life, we will encounter more crosses than if we just live in the world. This is God's provision to purify us. There is a kind of false teaching going around that says, "In the world you have suffered so much. People are so crafty and cruel that if you go to church and you are with believers, that is paradise." Well, it is paradise disguised because this is the proving ground, the training ground that God has prepared for you. If you cannot stand your brothers and sisters, you cannot stand the Lord.

I have seen people who have known the Lord for years, who have advanced in the Lord, and yet they left the church and stopped meeting with God's people, because they could not stand the sufferings. They are all by themselves. They think they can go on like that, but eventually, there is a complete fall. It is sad. We need the protection of the body of Christ. We need the fellowship of our brothers and sisters. We need to be told, corrected, encouraged and confirmed by our brothers and sisters. Do not think because you know something, that it must be right. You may be wrong. Be humble enough to be corrected. Be willing to be corrected and helped. Thank God, that is a provision He has provided for us. And I do hope that we will really make good use of it.

Paul's Exhortation

Finally, with all these problems we face, what should our final attitude be? Are we being so discouraged that we just give up? It is no use because the world is just full of lies. The world itself is under the greatest liar—Satan. And even in the church it seems to not be much better. Should we give up?

What is Paul's exhortation? That is the verse we read in the very beginning. He ends this chapter with a very positive attitude. "So then ..." In spite of all these false teachings, difficulties, trials—"So then, my beloved brethren, be firm [do not be moved], immovable [if you stand in Christ, if you stand in the word of God, if you stand in the teaching of the Holy Spirit, if you stand in the body of Christ], abounding always in the work of the Lord [it is not that you do not labor for the Lord anymore because of all these problems but work harder], knowing that your toil is not in vain in the Lord" (I Corinthians 15:58).

Then it says in chapter 16:13: "Be vigilant; watchful, stand fast in the faith; quit yourselves like men; be strong." Wonderful!

In Jude 24-25: "But to him that is able to keep you without stumbling, and to set you with exultation blameless before his glory, to the only God our Saviour, through Jesus Christ our Lord, be glory, majesty, might, and authority, from before the whole age, and now, and to all the ages. Amen" Praise the Lord!

10—The Basics of Giving

I Corinthians 16:1-2—Now concerning the collection for the saints, as I directed the assemblies of Galatia, so do ye do also. On the first of the week let each of you put by at home, laying up in whatever degree he may have prospered, that there may be no collections when I come.

II Corinthians 8:9—For ye know the grace of our Lord Jesus Christ, that for your sakes he, being rich, became poor, in order that ye by his poverty might be enriched.

II Corinthians 9:7—Each according as he is purposed in his heart; not grievingly, or of necessity; for God loves a cheerful giver.

We have mentioned that the Corinthian church had lots of problems. Even though they were saved by the grace of the Lord Jesus, they continued to live in their flesh. Their carnality was their biggest problem. Carnality is the very opposite of our calling. So I Corinthians begins with a wonderful, glorious calling: "God is faithful, by whom ye have been called into the fellowship of his Son Jesus Christ our Lord" (v. 9). In other words, the fellowship God the Father and God the Son have shared equally together, unselfishly, fully, completely with each other in the Spirit, from eternity, has been extended to believers. We are being included in the richness and fullness of the fellowship of the Father and the Son. Just think of that! What a calling that is! And carnality is the greatest reason why this fellowship is not full.

Even though the church in Corinth was full of problems, yet the apostle Paul took a positive approach. In other words, he is trying to show us what that fellowship is so that we may be delivered from everything that is low, contradictory, unholy, and displeasing to God.

When you come to the end of chapter 14, I feel like it is almost the end of that letter because Paul said, "Let everything be done comelily and with order." If everything among God's people can be done comelily, beautifully, harmoniously, peacefully, with one accord, with one spirit, with one mind, even with one speech, and there is a divine order among them, what more can be said? But then there are two more chapters following. One chapter is on this matter of resurrection. In other words, among the Corinthian believers, there were some who did not believe in resurrection, and it was a direct attack on the very meaning of the gospel of Jesus Christ. Therefore, Paul reiterated the meaning of the gospel.

Christ died for our sins according to the Scriptures. He was buried and then raised from the dead, and He appeared to a number of people to show that He is alive. And because He lives, we live also; and that is very important.

We have also fellowshipped together on this matter of false teachings because, throughout church history, there has always been false teaching. Wherever there is truth, there is falsehood. We can even put it another way. Where there is falsehood, there must be truth somewhere. And it is very, very important for God's people, especially in these last days, to be vigilant and watchful, to be faithful to the word of God and faithful to the Spirit of God who will explain His word to us.

Furthermore, we need the protection of the body of Christ, and that is the blessing of fellowship.

Collections

Following chapter 15, you would think that I Corinthians should be ended, but strangely Paul mentioned this matter of collections. Now I do not personally believe that the Corinthian church asked Paul about that question even though the Bible says, "Now concerning the collection." It is not something that the Corinthian church asked Paul about because due to their carnality, even though Paul mentioned this in their midst in the beginning, and they responded, yet they did not fulfill it. So Paul tried to mention this matter of collections again.

The Spirit of Giving

We know that this is something always in the heart of Paul. Paul always had in his heart the poor because this is the Spirit of Christ. It is said of our Lord Jesus in Isaiah 61:1a: "The Spirit of God is upon me, and He has anointed Me to preach the glad tidings to the meek." The fulfillment of this is in Luke 4, and that was at the beginning of our Lord's ministry in Galilee. He went into the synagogue in Nazareth, and they gave Him the book of Isaiah, and He read from chapter 61:1: "The Spirit of the Lord is upon Me, and He has anointed Me to preach the glad tidings to the poor." It is the very Spirit of Christ that He always remembered the poor, and as a servant of the Lord, Paul had the same burden in his heart.

You remember in Acts 15, after that Jerusalem council, the three pillars of the church in Jerusalem—Peter, James, and John—gave their right hand of fellowship to Barnabas and Paul and said to them, "We go to the Jewish nation, and you go to the uncircumcised, to the nations, but always remember the poor." And Paul said, "This is something that I was always diligent in doing" (see Galatians 2:9-10). Paul's heart was always to remember the poor.

At the beginning of church history, there was a prophet by the name of Agabus who came down from Jerusalem to Antioch (see Acts 11). He prophesied that there would be a great famine over the whole habitable world, and it happened at the time of Claudius. The church in Antioch gathered relief and sent it to Jerusalem by the hands of Barnabas and Paul. So later on, whenever Paul went on his missionary trips, he always tried to help God's people, especially the Gentiles, to think of the poor in Jerusalem. He did that in Galatia, in Achaia, and in Macedonia. So here he mentioned this matter of collections because, at that time, the believers in Jerusalem and in the Judean country seemed to be in poverty, and the churches in the Gentile world seemed to be more prosperous. Paul always reminded the believers everywhere to remember the poor, and he took collections for them.

Evidently, when he was first in Corinth, he mentioned this matter to the believers, and in their first love, in their zeal, they promised that they would do it. But unfortunately, because they continued to live in their own flesh, they soon forgot it. That is the reason, towards the end of I Corinthians, Paul had to remind them about this matter of collections, and he even suggested to them a systematic way of giving. That is to help people who do not have the habit of giving or who tend to forget it. Paul said, "Now why is it that you do not do it this way every first day of the week? (That is the day God's people meet.) You lay aside at your home a part of that which the Lord has prospered you, so when I come, I do not need to collect it."

Did the Corinthian believers respond? Not at all! Even after he reminded them of the collection they had promised, they did not do it. Not only did they not do it, but in II Corinthians 11, you find that there were some false apostles and wicked workers transforming themselves into the apostles of Jesus Christ. And they enticed the Corinthian believers away from Paul and Christ, and unto themselves. In other words, they not only did not listen to Paul, but many of them began to despise Paul and reject him, and Paul wrote a strong letter to them. Then he sent Titus to them, and through his ministry, thank God, they repented according to God, and eventually, he was able to share with them this matter of Christian giving as we find in II Corinthians.

So instead of focusing on special collections for special needs, we will just go to the very basics of Christian giving. Christian giving is very, very important, not only to our personal life but even to our life of fellowship. I would like to present it in the simplest way I can by asking four questions. Number one: why give? Number two: what is giving? Number three: how do you give? Number four: where do you give?

1—Why Give?

What is the reason that Christians should grow in the habit of giving? So far as human nature is concerned, giving is not natural. "Yes," we say, "give but give to me." We are thinking about ourselves. That is human nature. Giving out or giving away is our loss. We do not like it. Therefore we need to know why we should give. It is very simple. We give because God is the greatest giver. That is His character. You remember in James 1:17 it says, "Every good gift and every perfect gift comes down from above, from the Father of lights, with whom is no variation nor shadow of turning." Every good gift and every perfect gift comes down from above, from the God of lights, with whom is no variation. This means that it is constant, always giving, and there is no shadow of turning or refusing to give. That is our God.

I think there is one text that will tell us everything about giving, and that is John 3:16: "God so loved the world that He gave His only begotten Son, that whosoever believes in Him shall not perish but have everlasting life." That is the way God gives. He gives because He loves to give, and He gives everything. He even gave His only begotten Son. "He who spared not His only begotten Son, will He withhold anything from us" (see Romans 8:32). That is our God, and that is the very Spirit of our Lord Jesus.

The Grace of Our Lord Jesus

"For ye know the grace of our Lord Jesus Christ, that for your sakes he, being rich, became poor, in order that ye by his poverty might be enriched" (II Corinthians 8:9).

When you think of the grace of our Lord Jesus, how do you describe it? It is not something vague; it is something very real, very living. He said, "You know the grace of our Lord Jesus Christ." What is the grace of our Lord Jesus Christ? "For your sake, for our sake He, being rich ..." How can you describe the richness of Christ? All the fullness of the

Godhead dwells in Him bodily. You cannot describe it. It is infinite. All the glory, the honor, the power, the love, righteousness, holiness, separateness, fullness, all the unsearchable riches of Christ is the way Paul put it, and for our sakes, He became poor. He was willing to give up all His riches to be that poor carpenter of Nazareth. He was willing even to give up His own life to be crucified on Calvary's cross. He gave His all. He, who is the richest person I would say in the whole universe, voluntarily became the poorest person in the world, born in a manger, buried in a stranger's tomb. He became nothing that by His poverty we might be enriched. If our Lord Jesus were to keep His riches, we would be in poverty forever, but He was willing to become poor to enrich us. That is giving. That is the spirit of giving. And if there is no other reason why Christians should have the habit of giving, I think one reason is enough—the very nature and character of God and the Lord Jesus and what He has done for us. We have received from Him such riches, such mercy, and such grace. Should we not respond with the little that we are able in order to express our appreciation and at the same time to acknowledge that everything belongs to Him? We know that everything comes from Him, and we are grateful. Hence, we want to express it and acknowledge that without Him, we would have nothing. We want to have the same spirit as His, and that is why Christians give.

Old Testament Tithes and Offerings

In Genesis 14, after Abraham had won a big victory and delivered Lot from the four kings, he received many spoils. Melchisedec, the king of Salem, the king of righteousness, the high priest of God, came forward, served Abraham with bread and wine, and reminded him that it is God who gave him that victory. And Abraham took one-tenth of all the spoil and gave it to Melchisedec. In other words, he acknowledged that his victory came from God and not from himself. Everything was given to him by God, and he gave one-tenth to express his gratitude.

In Genesis 28, Jacob, that supplanter, was fleeing from his home. In the wilderness, He was so tired that he laid his head on a stone and slept. God appeared to him and said, "I am the God of your father. I am going to bless you and increase your seed which will bless all the nations. I will give the land to you." Jacob woke up, and he was frightened. He said, "Surely Jehovah is in this place, and I knew it not. … How dreadful is this place! this is none other but the house of God, and this is the gate of heaven" (Genesis 28:16-17). Then he made a vow and bargained with God. He could not even imagine the immensity of God's love and grace. He was so limited by his own little love and grace. So he said, "Now God, if you will keep me all the way, give me clothes to wear and food to eat and allow me to come back safely, then you will be my God, and I will give you one-tenth." Even with this, there was at least some appreciation from Jacob, but, of course, it was on condition.

When you come to the end of Leviticus in chapter 27:30-34, we see that God put them under the Law, and they had to give one-tenth—one-tenth of their land, one-tenth of the produce of the land, one-tenth of all the fruits of the trees, and one-tenth of all their domestic animals, without fault. Under the Law, they were required to give one-tenth to show two things—to make them realize that everything comes from God and to set apart one-tenth to give to God as a kind of appreciation. But the children of Israel rebelled against God, and one of the things they forgot was their tithes.

In the last book of the Old Testament, Malachi 3, God said: "Why do you rob Me?" They said, "Where do we rob You?" God said, "You rob Me of My tithes, which is one-tenth, and heave offerings, which are love offerings, and more than one-tenth." In other words, if an Israelite was faithful to the Lord and loved God with his heart, he gave at least two tenths, one-tenth for the tithe and, over and above it, a heave offering, which was a love offering and all the other kinds of offerings. God said, "Bring your whole tithe to My treasure house that there will be food in My house, and I will open the window of heaven until you cannot contain it." That is the Old Testament.

New Testament Giving

When you come to the New Testament, praise God, there is no requirement of one-tenth. Are you happy about it? You cannot find anywhere in the New Testament that God demands one-tenth, so you can keep it all—right? Not at all! It is just the opposite because we are not under law; we are now under grace. You think that since you are not under law, you can now be lawless. No, being under grace demands your all. Under the Law, you are required only one-tenth, but under grace, it is your all.

Romans 12:1 says, "Brethren, by the mercies of God I beseech you to present your bodies." It is not just a limb but your whole body which represents your whole being—what you are, what you have, what you shall be—everything. "Present your bodies a living sacrifice, holy, acceptable to God. It is your spiritual worship and reasonable service."

Under law there is a requirement of one-tenth, but under grace, it is the spirit of giving. God does not require you to give one-tenth. God said, "Where is My Spirit in you? Do you have the same Spirit as Mine? I have given My life to you, and that life has a nature. It is a nature of giving, not of keeping but of giving. So God said, "Now it is not a matter of one-tenth; it is a matter of ten tenths. Present your bodies a living sacrifice." Your whole being is given back to God as an expression of acknowledging that God has given you everything, and it is your response and your appreciation of Him. It is not a requirement, nor is it a demand of law. On the other hand, it is a beseeching or a begging from God. God begs you. If you are moved by His love and constrained by His mercies, what else can you do? You are His—altogether His. That is the spirit of giving. Are you willing to become poor that others may be enriched? That is the reason behind giving.

2—What is Giving?

I am afraid our whole concept of giving is wrong. In II Corinthians chapters 8-9, when the apostle Paul mentioned giving, he used a few special words that we would never connect with giving. The first word he mentioned in this matter of giving is grace. Chapter 8:4 says, "Begging of us with much entreaty to give effect to the grace and fellowship of the service which was to be rendered to the saints." "So that we begged Titus that, according as he had before begun, so he would also complete as to you this grace also" (v. 6).

Giving is Grace

Throughout this chapter and the next, you find the right interpretation or meaning of Christian giving is grace. This word, *grace,* according to the Greek, carries three meanings. Number one is the object of grace. Number two is the expression of grace. Number three is the response of grace.

Grace is something so gracious and so beautiful that it draws out from you joy, a pleasant feeling. That is grace. Therefore God is grace. Christ is full of grace. When we look at Him, He is so beautiful, so gracious, so attractive that He draws out from us an adoration, a love towards Him. That is grace.

Then grace is an expression because when something is done freely, openly (without condition), gladly, cheerfully, universally, that is the way God gives. That is the way grace is expressed.

And there is the response of grace. Those who have received grace should be gracious. You remember the parable our Lord Jesus used, how a servant owed his master a tremendous, immense amount that he could never pay back. Yet when the master forgave him, he went out and found another bondservant and choked his throat and said, "Pay." It was only a small amount, but he put him in prison. And the master said, "If you are not gracious, then grace is withheld; you go to prison." That is what grace is.

Now think of God. He is grace; He is beautiful to behold. He gives freely without condition and universally. His grace should touch our hearts and transform us that we also will be gracious. So giving is grace. So far as we are concerned, we receive such grace from God. How can we not be gracious too? And how do we express our graciousness? We express our graciousness by giving, not withholding, not taking but giving. So you find first of all that giving is the grace of our Lord Jesus Christ. "He who is rich became poor for us that by His poverty we might be enriched" (see II Corinthians 8:9).

Giving is Blessing

In the Scriptures, giving is also described as blessing. You will think that receiving is blessing. Who would think that giving is blessing? But God looks at it very differently. It is "more blessed to give than to receive" (Acts 20:35) because God is the one who always blesses and who always gives. So to Him giving is blessing. He blesses us by giving His only begotten Son. It is a blessing. When we give, we think we will lose something. I will be reduced because blessing is an increase but giving is a decrease. How can it be a blessing?

In the word of God, He used a parable. He said, "Giving is like sowing a seed." When the farmer sows his seed, by all outward appearance, he is losing. Sowing it, he loses, but if he does not sow, he cannot reap. And if he sows sparingly, he will reap sparingly. If he sows liberally, he will reap liberally. So the Bible says that giving is like sowing, and therefore it is a blessing. During famine time, if a farmer holds onto all the grain and says, "I need it; I need to eat it," and he refuses to sow, he will die quicker. When he sows, his heart is broken because he could not see it, but he has to wait until there is a harvest. So the word says, "If you sow sparingly, you will reap sparingly. If you sow liberally, you will reap bountifully." That is giving, and it is a blessing. The more you hold back, the less you will have. And that is all you will have. But when you give, God will give you more because He sees that you are trustworthy, and then you can give more. It is a blessing.

Giving is Fellowship

Giving is also fellowship. In I Corinthians 8, we see that it is grace and fellowship or sharing. God does not want us to be an individualist, thinking only of ourselves. He put us in the body of Christ. He wants us to share what He has blessed us with, and the more we share, the more He is able to supply us so that we can share more. The more we withhold, the less it will become. It is not only in the matter of material things; it is the same way in spiritual things. You will be like the Dead Sea, receiving all the time and never giving. In the Dead Sea, nothing can live. We are to be like the Jordan—whatever is received, we give out. It is living, and it is running. What is the blessing of fellowship? The blessing of fellowship is that not only are we set free, but others are enriched. Because we are willing to give, God can entrust us with more, and those who have received will bless God for us. Isn't that a wonderful blessing all around? What a fellowship that must be! Our whole concept of giving is so confined by our human frailty. May God open our understanding to see that it is grace, it is blessing, and it is fellowship.

3—How Do We Give?

Give Yourself to the Lord

II Corinthians chapters 8-9 tell us that, first of all, we give ourselves to the Lord just as the Macedonians did. They were in deep poverty, yet they had such a Spirit of Christ in them. They wanted to have a share in the service for their brothers in Jerusalem who lacked. So they asked that they might have a share in it. "But they gave themselves first to the Lord, and then they gave to us."

So how do we give? If we do not give ourselves to the Lord first, then even if we give, God is not pleased with it because it is not out of Him; it is out of ourselves. Some people may be naturally more generous, but that does not mean that when they give, God will be pleased with it. It has to come out of His life. Therefore, first of all, give yourself to the Lord. Anyone who does not give himself to the Lord, the Lord says, "You do not need to give. You can keep it for yourself." So how do you give? Give yourself to the Lord.

Give in Secret

Then we are to give in secret. In Matthew 6, our Lord Jesus said, "Do not give like the hypocrites. When they give, they blow the trumpets in the treasury as well as on the streets. 'See I am giving.'" That is the way the world gives. They give to have a name. The Lord says that they have their return. When you give, do not let your left hand know what your right hand is doing. You say that is impossible. How can my left hand not know what my right hand is doing, or my right hand not know what my left hand is doing since it is me? It is a metaphorical saying. It means to give secretly as unto the Lord. You do not give to man nor to a cause, but you give it to God. You are not asking for a return, such as having your name in the newspaper. You give it as unto the Lord. Now sometimes, I know it is impossible to be an unknown giver, but try to be an unknown giver as much as you can. But even when you may be known, do not take it as your credit because all you give is from the Lord and not from you. That is the spirit of giving in secret.

Give Cheerfully

Then we are to give cheerfully because God loves a cheerful giver. It is not to be done grudgingly or as though something is squeezed out of us or as something we are forced to do, and we do it grievously. We are to do it gladly and joyfully. God loves a cheerful giver. You may give to the extent of weeping, but in your heart, there is joy.

Give What You Have

And God said, "Give what you have, not what you do not have." You do not need to borrow in order to give. What He has given you, you gladly give. It is not compulsory. God does not require that we have to give one-tenth, but can we do less than what the Law requires? There is no law and nothing to be forced. Everything is according to our relationship with the Lord. If we really understood what giving is, I am afraid many of us may have to change our lifestyle. We say we have nothing to give: "My family and I need every penny of it. I cannot give anything." If you cannot give anything, God will say, "You do not need to give. That's okay; you are not under law; you are under grace." But look at your lifestyle. The way we live needs to be changed. Oftentimes, it is the poor who give, not the rich. God have mercy on us.

Give Systematically

And then, for the sake of some who may be weak, give systematically. What the Lord has prospered you, set apart something in order to help cultivate the habit of giving. So that is how you give.

4—Where Do You Give?

Spiritual Exercise

Giving is a spiritual exercise; therefore, it is more than just a matter of giving. You learn a lot before God by giving. It is something that you have to go to the Lord and ask Him, "Where should my giving go?" It is not just according to the needs because needs are everywhere. How do you know where to give the little that you are entrusted with? It is a spiritual exercise. It is a serious thing, and you really need to exercise it before God. Suppose God gave me one dollar. It does not mean if I throw it away, I have solved the problem and done my duty. That is not the way of giving. What God has given to you is a trust. You are a steward; hence you need to know the mind of the Master in how to use that money. So it is not a careless throwing away. You have to exercise before the Lord. Nobody is going to tell you where to give. On the other hand, you have to seek the Lord about it so you know where it should go. Pray about it. Seek the Lord about it. It is not that whenever you see a need, then you give, but the real need that is your responsibility you are not fulfilling. You have to pray; it is a spiritual exercise.

Give to the House of God

But there are certain things we should remember. In the Old Testament time, the Lord said, "Bring your tithes into the treasure house that My house may have food." In other words, translated into New Testament terms, we are in an assembly together, and there is a responsibility for us to give. We need to give to the assembly because giving is more than just an individual thing. It is a corporate thing. So when we give to the Lord through the church, then the church as a corporate being will seek the Lord as to where that fund should go. It is a corporate thing. So we do not need to forget the house of God. Oftentimes, we make giving such an individual thing. We will decide where the money is to go and let the house of God be desolate. But you are using the facilities, you are enjoying all the good of it, and you never take any responsibility. That is wrong and unrighteous. So that is something we need to understand. There is the house of God that we need to give to, and, of course, it is not just for maintenance. The house of God is to give to the Lord's work, to the poor, and to all the needs for the gospel. There are many needs everywhere. The demand is great. With all the modern techniques people use to get some money out of our pockets, we need to be exercised carefully before the Lord that we may be trustworthy stewards of God.

Let us look to the Lord that by His grace, we may have the spirit of giving fall on us and be gracious as He is.

TITLES AVAILABLE
from Christian Fellowship Publishers
By Stephen Kaung

Abiding in God
Acts—*The Working of the Holy Spirit*
"But We See Jesus"—*The Life of the Lord Jesus*
Discipled to Christ—*As Seen in the Life of Simon Peter*
Elijah and Elisha—*One Prophetic Ministry*
God's Purpose for the Family
Government and Ministry in the Local Church
The Gymnasium of Christ
In the Footsteps of Christ
Isaiah—*The Redemption of the Lord*
The Key to "Revelation" – Vol. 1
The Key to "Revelation" – Vol. 2
The Master's Training
Men After God's Own Heart
Ministering the Word of God
Moses, the Servant of God
Nehemiah—*Recovering the Testimony of God*
New Covenant Living & Ministry
Now We See the Church—*the Life of the Church, the Body of Christ*
Proverbs—*Wisdom Builds God's House*
Recovery
Shepherding
Teach Us to Pray
The Songs of Degrees—*Meditations on Fifteen Psalms*
The Sons of Korah
The Splendor of His Ways—*Seeing the Lord's End in Job*
Titus
Worship

The "God Has Spoken" Series
Seeing Christ in the Old Testament, Part One
Seeing Christ in the Old Testament, Part Two
Seeing Christ in the New Testament

Made in the USA
Monee, IL
13 August 2021